Cheesecakes

and Other Cheese Desserts

Cheesecakes

and Other Cheese Desserts

Mac Woo and June Lee

Marshall Cavendish
Cuisine

Dedication

To our family and friends, for their never-ending support in our venture.
Your feedback, contribution and encouragement have motivated us greatly,
and for that, we will strive to be even better.

Acknowledgements

One of our greatest enjoyments is to experiment with new and exciting flavours
of cheesecakes and pastries in our kitchen, and this project gave us the perfect
opportunity to indulge in our favourite pursuit.

We would like to thank the teams at Marshall Cavendish Cuisine and Elements By
The Box, for they have helped translate our love and passion into this wonderful
recipe collection. This is one of our greatest achievements by far, and we want
them to know that not a minute of their effort goes unappreciated. We are truly
fortunate and grateful to be able to collaborate with both teams. Their invaluable
friendship, advice and expertise have made the execution of this project
extremely successful, resulting in this book worthy to be cherished
and used by all baking enthusiasts.

Photographer : Joshua Tan, Elements By The Box
Designers   : Lynn Chin Nyuk Ling and Rachel Chen

First published as Crave: Cheese Desserts to Die For, 2006
This new edition 2011

Published by Marshall Cavendish Cuisine
An imprint of Marshall Cavendish International
1 New Industrial Road, Singapore 536196

Other Marshall Cavendish Offices:

Marshall Cavendish International. PO Box 65829 London EC1P 1NY, UK • Marshall Cavendish Corporation. 99 White Plains
Road, Tarrytown NY 10591-9001, USA • Marshall Cavendish International (Thailand) Co Ltd. 253 Asoke, 12th Flr, Sukhumvit 21
Road, Klongtoey Nua, Wattana, Bangkok 10110, Thailand • Marshall Cavendish (Malaysia) Sdn Bhd, Times Subang, Lot 46,
Subang Hi-Tech Industrial Park, Batu Tiga, 40000 Shah Alam, Selangor Darul Ehsan, Malaysia

Marshall Cavendish is a trademark of Times Publishing Limited

National Library Board Singapore Cataloguing in Publication Data

Woo, Mac, 1979-
Cheesecakes : and other cheese desserts / Mac Woo and June Lee. – Singapore : Marshall Cavendish Cuisine, c2011.
p. cm. ISBN : 978-981-4346-59-7

1. Cheesecake. 2. Desserts. I. Lee, June, 1979- II. Title.

TX773 641.8653 -- dc22   OCN704500887

Printed in Singapore by KWF Printing Pte Ltd

Contents

Preface

I discovered the art of baking through my maternal grandmother during my early teenage years. Whenever her desire to bake struck, I'd make sure I was there to watch her whip up her delicious breads, tarts and cakes. The first time I tried cheesecake, I thought it was the most heavenly dessert I'd ever tasted. It was in a class of its own—it seemed like the kind of dessert one could only find in chic and upscale restaurants or patisseries. I was determined to find out how to re-create this at home. Since my grandmother had never baked cheesecakes before, I knew I would definitely do her proud if I could pull it off.

After finally getting down to a recipe, I plucked up my courage and proceeded with my first baking project. It was surprisingly easy to put together, and when I shared it with my family, they (and certainly my grandmother) were impressed! My confidence grew and I began experimenting with different styles and flavours of cheesecakes over the years.

In varsity, I met Mac and we discovered our similar passions for desserts and especially cheesecakes. Although we were architecturally trained, we decided to pursue our passion and started an online joint venture selling cheesecakes and chocolate cakes. We spent much time and effort experimenting with different flavours and distributing samples to get suggestions on how to improve our cakes. Today, many customers order our cheesecakes for a wide variety of occasions, ranging from birthday and housewarming parties to office gatherings.

I recall the famous chef Mr. Thomas Keller saying, "...there is no such thing as perfect food..." I believe our quest for cheesecakes and desserts will never end. You can use these recipes again and again—for intimate gatherings, grand parties and soirées; as festive food gifts; or even for yourself whenever you need to satisfy your sweet tooth. Treat this collection of recipes as a guide to inspire you rather than an instructional blueprint, and inject your personality into these cheesecakes and desserts! We have also included brief sections on tips and techniques, essential ingredients and equipment at the back of this book. Do take some time to read them before you begin on your creations.

I'm sure you'll enjoy making these cheesecakes and desserts as much as we've enjoyed creating them. Baking is a therapeutic process, so allow your imagination and creativity to run wild!

Bon appétit!

June Lee

Perennial Favourites

Lemon Crumble Cheesecake Bars *15*

Warm Cheese Soufflés *6*

Three Citrus Cream Cheese Pound Cake *19*

Petite Choux with Cream Cheese Pastry Cream *20*

American Sour Cream Cheesecake *23*

Cream Cheese Sablé Sandwich Cookies with
  Creamy Peanut Butter Frosting *24*

Rum-Raisin and Walnut Frozen Cheesecake Terrine *27*

Caramel Cream Cheese Flans *28*

Sweet Ricotta Tart *31*

Lemon Crumble Cheesecake Bars

These old-fashioned bars, consisting of a zesty lemon cheese filling sandwiched between a crispy cinnamon crust and crumble, are ideal finger food for your party platter.

Cinnamon Crumble (for crust and topping)

Plain (all-purpose) flour	**210 g (7^1/$_2$ oz)**
Icing (confectioner's) sugar	**80 g (2^3/$_4$ oz)**
Ground cinnamon	**^{1}/$_2$ tsp**
Salt	**^{3}/$_4$ tsp**
Butter	**150 g (5^1/$_4$ oz), cold, cut into 2.5-cm (1-in) cubes**

Filling

Cream cheese	**520 g (1 lb 2^1/$_4$ oz)**
Castor (superfine) sugar	**150 g (5^1/$_4$ oz)**
Lemon juice	**3^1/$_3$ Tbsp**
Eggs	**2^1/$_2$, large, lightly beaten**
Lemon zest	**2^1/$_2$ tsp**

Garnish (optional)

Icing (confectioner's) sugar

Lemon zest

Line the bottom and sides of a 23-cm (9-in) square pan with aluminium foil, creating an overhang on each side. Butter foil.

Prepare crumble. In a blender (processor), briefly pulse flour, icing sugar, cinnamon and salt to mix. Add cold butter and pulse until mixture resembles coarse meal.

Sprinkle two-thirds of crumble into prepared pan and press into an even layer over the entire bottom. Refrigerate for 30 minutes. Keep remaining crumble chilled.

Preheat oven to 180°C (350°F). Bake crust for 15–20 minutes until lightly browned.

Prepare filling while crust is baking. With an electric mixer, beat cream cheese and sugar at medium speed until creamy. Add lemon juice and blend until smooth. Lower speed and add eggs, a little at a time, mixing until just incorporated. Fold in lemon zest.

Remove pan from oven and pour filling onto crust. Sprinkle remaining crumble evenly on top. Bake for 30 minutes, then reduce temperature to 160°C (325°F) and bake for another 20–30 minutes until crumble is golden brown and filling is set. Remove from oven and cool on a wire rack. Refrigerate for at least 6 hours.

Using foil extensions as handles, remove cheesecake from pan and cut into squares or bars. Dust with icing sugar and garnish with lemon zest before serving, if desired.

Makes nine 7.5-cm (3-in) squares or
eighteen 7.5 x 4-cm (3-in x 1½-in) bars.

Warm Cheese Soufflés

Folding whipped egg whites into the batter causes the soufflés to rise during baking, which contributes to their cotton-light and airy texture. They are best when served straight from the oven.

Butter	**1 Tbsp**
Plain (all-purpose) flour	**1 Tbsp**
Salt	**$^1/_4$ tsp**
Milk	**4 Tbsp**
Cream cheese	**115 g (4 oz), softened**
Vanilla essence	**$^3/_4$ tsp**
Eggs	**2, whites and yolks separated**
Sugar	**65 g (2$^1/_4$ oz)**
Cocoa powder	**for dusting**

Place six 8.5-cm (3$^1/_2$-in) wide and 4.5-cm (1$^2/_3$-in) high ramekins on a baking tray. Set aside.

In a small saucepan, melt the butter over low heat. Stir in flour and salt. Gradually add milk, stirring constantly until thickened. Stir in softened cream cheese and vanilla essence until smooth. Remove from heat and set aside.

Preheat oven to 160°C (325°F).

In a small bowl, beat egg yolks with half the sugar until thickened and pale yellow. Fold into cream cheese mixture and cool slightly.

In a separate, clean mixing bowl, whisk egg whites with an electric mixer at medium speed until foamy. Increase speed to high and gradually add remaining sugar. Whisk until firm and glossy peaks form. Gently fold into cream cheese mixture until just incorporated.

Divide batter evenly among ramekins. Bake for 18–20 minutes, or until well risen and tops are lightly browned. Dust with cocoa powder and serve immediately.

For a more decadent treat, make a hole in the centre of each soufflé and pour in a generous amount of chocolate sauce (see pg 151).

Makes 6 soufflés

Three Citrus Cream Cheese Pound Cake

Rich, dense and buttery, this pound cake is simply delicious, even on its own. Jazz it up with a generous dollop of sweetened whipped cream and fresh fruit, if desired.

Cake flour	185 g ($6^1/_2$ oz)
Bicarbonate of soda	$^1/_8$ tsp
Salt	$^1/_8$ tsp
Butter	150 g ($5^1/_3$ oz), softened but still cool
Cream cheese	135 g ($4^3/_4$ oz)
Castor (superfine) sugar	220 g ($7^3/_4$ oz)
Eggs	3, large
Vanilla essence	$^2/_3$ tsp
Lime juice	2 Tbsp
Orange zest	$^1/_2$ tsp
Lemon zest	$^1/_2$ tsp
Lime zest	$^1/_2$ tsp

Preheat oven to 160°C (325°F). Grease bottom and sides of a 23 x 10 x 7-cm (9 x 4 x 3-in) loaf pan and line bottom with baking paper.

Sift together cake flour, baking soda and salt. Set aside.

With an electric mixer, beat butter and cream cheese at medium speed until smooth, about 30 seconds. Gradually add sugar and beat for 3–4 minutes until light and fluffy, scraping the bowl occasionally.

Add eggs, 1 at a time, beating well after each addition.

Beat in vanilla essence and lime juice. Lower speed and add flour mixture in 3 additions, beating until just incorporated after each addition.

Fold in orange, lemon and lime zests by hand.

Transfer batter into loaf pan and level top with a spatula. Bake for 1 hour 30 minutes–1 hour 40 minutes, or until top of loaf turns golden brown and a metal skewer inserted into the centre comes out clean.

Cool in pan for 10 minutes. Remove cake from pan and cool on a wire rack. Store airtight for up to 3 days at room temperature or in the refrigerator for up to 1 week.

Makes a 23 x 10-cm (9 x 4-in) loaf cake

Petite Choux with Cream Cheese Pastry Cream

These crisp yet tender mini puffs ooze with velvety smooth cream cheese pastry cream.

Cream Cheese Pastry Cream

Egg	$^1/_2$, **large**
Egg yolks	**3, large**
Plain (all-purpose) flour	**1$^1/_4$ Tbsp**
Corn flour (cornstarch)	**1$^1/_4$ Tbsp**
Castor (superfine) sugar	**70 g (2$^1/_2$ oz)**
Milk	**150 ml (5 fl oz)**
Whipping cream	**150 ml (5 fl oz)**
Vanilla essence	$^2/_3$ **tsp**
Cream cheese	**145 g (5 oz), softened**

Petite Choux Dough

Milk	**3 Tbsp**
Water	**3 Tbsp**
Unsalted butter	**2$^1/_3$ Tbsp, diced**
Salt	**a pinch**
Plain (all-purpose) flour	**45 g (1$^1/_2$ oz)**
Eggs	**1$^1/_2$, large, lightly beaten**

Prepare pastry cream. In a medium bowl, beat egg, egg yolks, flour, corn flour and 1 Tbsp sugar until pale yellow.

In a medium saucepan, heat milk, whipping cream and remaining sugar over medium heat until just about to boil. Slowly whisk into egg mixture then return mixture to saucepan and cook over low heat, stirring constantly, until thickened and smooth. Remove from heat and stir in vanilla essence.

Transfer pastry cream to another bowl and cover with plastic wrap. Cool, then refrigerate for 4 hours. Beat softened cream cheese into chilled pastry cream until smooth. Cover and refrigerate for an additional hour.

Prepare petite choux dough. In a medium saucepan, warm milk, water, butter and salt over medium heat until boiling. Remove from heat, add flour and stir vigorously until blended. Return to heat and continue stirring until mixture leaves the sides of saucepan and forms a ball. Remove from heat. Let stand for 2–3 minutes.

Whisk in eggs in 3 additions, making sure each addition is fully incorporated before adding the next. The dough should be smooth and shiny.

Preheat oven to 210°C (410°F). Line baking trays with baking paper.

Transfer dough into a pastry bag fitted with a 1-cm ($^1/_2$-in) tip. Pipe dollops 2.5-cm (1-in) in diameter, 5-cm (2-in) apart. Bake for 15 minutes. Remove from oven and prick sides of each puff with a sharp knife. This will help create a hollow in the puffs.

Reduce temperature to 185°C (365°F). Return puffs to oven, prop open door and bake a further 10–12 minutes, or until puffs are golden brown. Transfer puffs to a wire rack to cool.

To assemble, slice each puff horizontally in the middle, three-quarter way through. Spoon or pipe chilled pastry cream inside. Serve immediately or keep puffs refrigerated before serving.

Makes about thirty 4-cm (1$^1/_2$-in) cream puffs

American Sour Cream Cheesecake

Considered the ne plus ultra of all cheesecakes, this legendary favourite has won the hearts of many cheesecake purists. A layer of tangy sour cream topping completes this tall and velvety smooth baked cheesecake.

Base

Digestive biscuits	**165 g ($5^3/_4$ oz), finely ground**
Light brown sugar	**$1^1/_2$ Tbsp**
Butter	**3 Tbsp, melted and still warm**

Filling

Cream cheese	**545 g (1 lb $3^1/_4$ oz)**
Castor (superfine) sugar	**120 g ($4^1/_4$ oz)**
Plain (all-purpose) flour	**$1^3/_4$ Tbsp, sifted**
Vanilla essence	**$2/_3$ tsp**
Lemon zest	**$1^1/_4$ tsp**
Eggs	**3, large**
Whipping cream	**4 Tbsp**

Sour Cream Topping

Sour cream	**250 ml (8 fl oz / 1 cup)**
Castor (superfine) sugar	**$1^1/_2$ tsp**
Vanilla essence	**$2/_3$ tsp**

Strawberry or blueberry pie filling (optional)

Prepare base. Mix together digestives, light brown sugar and warm melted butter. Press firmly onto the bottom and 2.5-cm (1-in) up the sides of an 18-cm (7-in) round springform pan. Refrigerate for 1 hour.

Preheat oven to 150°C (300°F).

Prepare filling. With an electric mixer, beat cream cheese and sugar at medium speed until creamy. Beat in sifted flour, vanilla essence and lemon zest until smooth. Lower speed and add eggs, 1 at a time, mixing until just incorporated. Gradually add whipping cream until well mixed.

Pour filling onto prepared base. Bake in a water bath for 1 hour 20 minutes–1 hour 40 minutes, or until edge of filling is almost set and centre is slightly wobbly.

For topping, stir together sour cream, sugar and vanilla essence until smooth. Remove cheesecake from oven, spread sour cream mixture evenly on top and return to the oven.

Lower temperature to 130°C (270°F) and bake for another 20–25 minutes. Turn oven off and leave cheesecake inside for 30 minutes with oven door closed. Open oven door and leave cheesecake for another 30 minutes. Remove cheesecake from oven and cool on a wire rack.

Refrigerate for at least 6 hours before unmoulding and serving. Top with strawberry or blueberry pie filling, if desired.

Makes an 18-cm (7-in) round cheesecake

Cream Cheese Sablé Sandwich Cookies with Creamy Peanut Butter Frosting

Nothing beats the simple goodness of these buttery sablé cookies enriched with cream cheese. Dip the cookies in melted chocolate or chocolate fondue sauce, or enjoy them, sans frosting, with a good cup of tea or coffee.

Cream Cheese Cookie Dough

Plain (all-purpose) flour	**250 g ($8^3/_4$ oz)**
Salt	**$^1/_4$ tsp**
Butter	**170 g (6 oz), softened but still cool**
Cream cheese	**85 g (3 oz)**
Castor (superfine) sugar	**150 g ($5^1/_4$ oz)**
Lemon zest	**1 Tbsp**

Peanut Butter Frosting

Creamy peanut butter	**70 g ($2^1/_2$ oz)**
Butter	**30 g (1 oz), softened**
Icing (confectioner's) sugar	**300 g ($10^1/_2$ oz)**
Milk	**3–4 Tbsp**
Dark chocolate	**45 g ($1^1/_2$ oz), finely chopped**

Prepare cookie dough. In a bowl, stir together flour and salt. Set aside.

With an electric mixer, beat butter, cream cheese and sugar at medium speed until light and fluffy. Mix in lemon zest until well incorporated.

Lower speed and gradually add flour mixture until just incorporated and dough comes together in a ball. Roll dough into 2 logs, each 4-cm ($1^1/_2$-in) in diameter.

Cover with plastic wrap and refrigerate for at least 3 hours. Dough can be stored for up to 4 weeks in the freezer.

Preheat oven to 180°C (350°F).

Working with 1 log at a time, unwrap and cut into 0.5-cm ($^1/_4$-in) thick slices with a sharp knife. Place cookies 2.5-cm (1-in) apart on an ungreased baking tray.

Bake for 16–19 minutes, or until edges are lightly browned. Stand cookies for 1 minute before transferring to wire racks to cool.

Make peanut butter frosting. Blend peanut butter and softened butter well. Alternately add icing sugar and milk, mixing until smooth. Mix in chopped chocolate.

Spread a layer of frosting on a cookie and sandwich with another cookie. Repeat to make 30–35 sandwich cookies.

Store frosted cookies in an airtight container for up to 3 days.

Makes 30–35 sandwich cookies

Rum-Raisin and Walnut Frozen Cheesecake Terrine

Who doesn't enjoy a little rum and raisin ice cream now and then? This cheesecake terrine comes very close to the original, with a handful of toasted walnuts thrown in for extra crunch.

Rum-soaked Raisins	
Dark raisins	**85 g (3 oz)**
Dark rum	**2³/₄ Tbsp**
Filling	
Cream cheese	**345 g (12¹/₄ oz)**
Castor (superfine) sugar	**110 g (4 oz)**
Rum essence	**²/₃ tsp**
Milk	**4 Tbsp**
Whipping cream	**345 ml (11 fl oz)**
Walnuts	**50 g (1³/₄ oz), toasted and coarsely chopped**

Prepare rum-soaked raisins. Toss raisins and dark rum together in a small bowl. Cover and leave for at least 2 hours or overnight in the refrigerator. Drain well before using.

Line the inside of a 23 x 10 x 7-cm (9 x 4 x 3-in) loaf pan with plastic wrap. Set aside.

Prepare filling. With an electric mixer, beat cream cheese and sugar at medium speed until smooth. Gradually beat in rum essence and milk until well incorporated.

In a separate mixing bowl, beat whipping cream until medium peaks form. Fold one-third of cream into cream cheese mixture. Gently fold in remaining cream until just incorporated. Fold in drained raisins and chopped walnuts.

Transfer mixture to lined loaf pan. Press mixture firmly down at the edges and four corners. Level top with a spatula and cover tightly with plastic wrap. Freeze at least 6 hours, or until firm.

To unmould, briefly use a hairdryer to blow hot air around the outside of pan. Remove top layer of plastic wrap and invert on a serving platter. Remove pan and remaining plastic wrap. Let stand at room temperature for 10 minutes before slicing and serving.

Decorate as desired. Store remaining terrine, covered, in the freezer.

Makes a 23 x 10-cm (9 x 4-in) terrine

Caramel Cream Cheese Flans

Often found on the menus of fine dining establishments, this rich and elegant cream cheese-enriched flan is effortless to whip up in your very own kitchen.

Caramel Base

Castor (superfine) sugar	**90 g (3¹/₄ oz)**
Lemon juice	**²/₃ tsp**

Flan Custard

Cream cheese	**125 g (4¹/₂ oz), softened**
Condensed milk	**130 g (4¹/₂ oz)**
Milk	**150 ml (5 fl oz)**
Eggs	**2, large**
Vanilla essence	**¹/₃ tsp**

Garnish (optional)

Sweetened whipped cream (see pg 152)	
Fresh berries	

Preheat oven to 145°C (290°F).

Prepare caramel base. In a small saucepan, boil sugar and lemon juice over medium-high heat for 5–7 minutes until medium amber in colour. Immediately pour into six 8.5-cm (3¹/₂-in) wide and 4.5-cm (1¹/₂-in) high ramekins and swirl to coat the bottoms. Set aside.

Prepare flan custard. In a blender (processor), blend cream cheese, condensed milk, milk, eggs and vanilla essence at medium speed until smooth. Strain and divide mixture evenly among ramekins.

Place ramekins in a deep roasting pan and pour boiling water into pan until halfway up the sides of ramekins. Bake for 40–45 minutes, or until set and a toothpick inserted into the centre of flan comes out almost clean.

Remove ramekins from water bath and cool. Refrigerate for at least 4 hours.

To unmould, set each ramekin in a shallow bowl of very hot water for 1–1¹/₂ minutes. Run a paring knife along the edge of flan. Invert onto a serving dish and shake ramekin to release.

Serve immediately, garnished with sweetened whipped cream and fresh berries, if desired.

Makes 6 flans

Sweet Ricotta Tart

Also known as "Torta di Ricotta", this recipe is a modern take on the traditional Italian favourite. This delicately textured tart is best made the day before serving to allow the flavours to ripen. Serve thin slices with freshly brewed espresso.

Sweet Crust Dough for a 23-cm (9-in) round (see pg 148)	1 portion
Filling	
Ricotta cheese	190 g (6³/₄ oz), well drained
Mascarpone cheese	115 g (4 oz)
Castor (superfine) sugar	75 g (2³/₄ oz)
Ground cinnamon	¹/₄ tsp
Plain (all-purpose) flour	2¹/₃ Tbsp
Eggs	2, medium
Dark rum	2 Tbsp
Lemon zest	1¹/₄ tsp
Orange zest	1¹/₄ tsp
Whipping cream	105 ml (3¹/₃ fl oz)
Candied mixed fruit	60 g (2 oz)

Butter and flour a 23-cm (9-in) tart pan with a removable bottom.

Prepare Sweet Crust Dough. On a floured surface, roll dough to approximately 0.5-cm (¹/₄-in) thick and large enough to line pan. Transfer dough to pan, lining bottom and sides evenly. Trim off excess dough with a paring knife. Prick base all over with a fork and refrigerate for at least 1 hour before using.

Preheat oven to 180°C (350°F).

Prepare filling. With an electric mixer, beat ricotta and mascarpone cheeses on medium speed until smooth. Add sugar, cinnamon and flour, mixing until well incorporated. Lower speed and add eggs, 1 at a time, beating until fully incorporated after each addition. Blend in dark rum, lemon zest and orange zest.

In a separate bowl, beat whipping cream until soft peaks form. Fold into cheese mixture until incorporated. Fold in candied mixed fruit.

Pour filling onto chilled crust. Bake for 45–50 minutes until filling is risen, golden brown and almost firm to the touch. Turn off oven and leave tart inside for 45 minutes with the door closed. Remove tart from oven and cool on a wire rack.

Remove tart pan and transfer tart to a serving platter. Refrigerate overnight. Decorate as desired before serving.

Makes a 23-cm (9-in) round tart

Chocolate

Dark Chocolate-Raspberry Cheesecake

Dark chocolate and raspberries, an increasingly popular flavour combination in cakes and confections, take centre stage in this luxurious baked cheesecake.

18-cm (7-in) round Oreo Crust (see pg 146)	**1**
Cream cheese	**450 g (16 oz)**
Castor (superfine) sugar	**70 g (2^1/$_2$ oz)**
Vanilla essence	**^{1}/$_3$ tsp**
Corn flour (cornstarch)	**2^1/$_2$ Tbsp, sifted**
Dark chocolate	**85 g (3 oz), melted**
Eggs	**2, large**
Whipping cream	**75 ml (2^1/$_2$ fl oz)**
Milk	**75 ml (2^1/$_2$ fl oz)**
Raspberry purée	**85 g (3 oz)**

Prepare round Oreo Crust.

Preheat oven to 160°C (325°F).

With an electric mixer, beat cream cheese and sugar at medium speed until creamy. Beat in vanilla essence, sifted corn flour and melted dark chocolate until smooth.

Lower speed and add eggs, 1 at a time, mixing until just incorporated. Gradually add whipping cream, milk and raspberry purée until well mixed.

Pour filling onto prepared crust. Bake in a water bath for 1 hour 10 minutes–1 hour 30 minutes, or until edge of filling is set and centre is slightly wobbly.

Turn off oven and leave cheesecake inside for 30 minutes with oven door closed. Prop open door and leave for another 30 minutes. Remove cheesecake from oven and cool on a wire rack.

Refrigerate for at least 6 hours before unmoulding. Decorate as desired before serving.

Makes an 18-cm (7-in) round cheesecake

Fudgy Chocolate-Cream Cheese Swirl Brownies

These incredibly fudgy brownies have a chocolate-cream cheese layer sandwiched in between. Enjoy them straight from the refrigerator or warmed and topped with a scoop of good vanilla ice cream.

Chocolate-cheese Filling

Dark chocolate	**50 g (1³/₄ oz), finely chopped**
Whipping cream	**2 Tbsp**
Cream cheese	**115 g (4 oz), softened**
Egg	**¹/₂, large, lightly beaten**
Plain (all-purpose) flour	**1 tsp**

Brownie Batter

Plain (all-purpose) flour	**130 g (4¹/₂ oz)**
Salt	**¹/₄ tsp**
Dark chocolate	**140 g (5 oz), chopped**
Butter	**95 g (3¹/₄ oz)**
Castor (superfine) sugar	**120 g (4¹/₄ oz)**
Light brown sugar	**120 g (4¹/₄ oz)**
Vanilla essence	**1¹/₂ tsp**
Eggs	**2¹/₂, large**
Icing (confectioner's) sugar (optional)	**for dusting**

Line the bottom and sides of an 18-cm (7-in) square pan with aluminium foil, creating an overhang on each side. Butter and flour base.

Preheat oven to 175°C (350°F).

Prepare chocolate-cheese filling. Place chopped chocolate and whipping cream in a heatproof bowl, set over a pot of simmering water and stir until completely melted and smooth. Remove from heat. (Alternatively, heat in a microwave oven at medium power until completely melted and smooth.) Leave to cool slightly.

Stir cream cheese until smooth. Blend in chocolate mixture until well mixed. Gradually add egg and flour, stirring until well incorporated. Set aside.

Prepare brownie batter. In a medium bowl, stir together flour and salt and set aside. Place chopped chocolate and butter in a heatproof bowl, set over a pot of simmering water and stir until completely melted and smooth. Remove from heat. (Alternatively, heat in a microwave oven at medium power until completely melted and smooth.) Stir in castor and light brown sugar, vanilla essence and eggs. Fold in flour mixture until just moistened.

Pour half of brownie batter into prepared pan. Spread chocolate cheese filling over evenly and almost to edge of pan. Cover with remaining brownie batter. Bake for 50–60 minutes, or until a toothpick inserted into the centre comes out with moist crumbs attached. Remove from oven and leave to cool in pan on a wire rack.

Using foil extensions as handles, remove brownie from pan. Cut into 4.5-cm (1³/₄-in) squares, dust with icing sugar and decorate as desired before serving. The brownies can be kept covered and refrigerated for up to 3 days.

Makes sixteen 4.5-cm (1³/₄-in) squares

Nutella Cheesecake

Nutella originated from Italy in the 1940s. This luscious and fragrant spread, which features the classic combination of chocolate and hazelnuts, is used to flavour this creamy cheesecake.

18-cm (7-in) round
  Oreo Crust
  (see pg 146)
	1

Filling	
Cream cheese	**450 g (16 oz)**
Light brown sugar	**3 Tbsp**
Vanilla essence	**$^1/_3$ tsp**
Corn flour (cornstarch)	**2$^1/_3$ Tbsp, sifted**
Chocolate hazelnut **spread (eg. Nutella)**	**150 g (5$^1/_4$ oz)**
Eggs	**2, large**
Whipping cream	**75 ml (2$^1/_2$ fl oz)**
Milk	**75 ml (2$^1/_2$ fl oz)**

Prepare round Oreo Crust.

Preheat oven to 160°C (325°F).

With an electric mixer, beat cream cheese and light brown sugar at medium speed until creamy. Beat in vanilla essence, sifted corn flour and chocolate hazelnut spread until smooth.

Lower speed and add eggs, 1 at a time, mixing until just incorporated. Gradually add whipping cream and milk until well mixed.

Pour filling onto prepared crust. Bake in a water bath for 1 hour 10 minutes–1 hour 30 minutes, or until edge of filling is set and centre is slightly wobbly.

Turn off oven and leave cheesecake inside for 30 minutes with oven door closed. Prop open door and leave for another 30 minutes. Remove cheesecake from oven and cool on a wire rack.

Refrigerate for at least 6 hours before unmoulding. Decorate as desired before serving.

Makes an 18-cm (7-in) round cheesecake

Chocolate-Macha Cheesecake

Macha, Japanese green tea powder, is widely used in Japanese desserts. Here, we've paired it with dark chocolate to produce a surprisingly pleasant and sophisticated flavour in this two-layer cheesecake.

18-cm (7-in) round Oreo Crust (see pg 146)	**1**
Water	**3 Tbsp**
Castor (superfine) sugar	**135 g (4^3/$_4$ oz)**
Japanese green tea powder	**1 Tbsp**
Cream cheese	**495 g (1 lb 1^1/$_2$ oz)**
Vanilla essence	**^{1}/$_3$ tsp**
Corn flour (cornstarch)	**2^1/$_2$ Tbsp, sifted**
Eggs	**2^1/$_2$, medium, lightly beaten**
Whipping cream	**80 ml (2^1/$_2$ fl oz)**
Milk	**80 ml (2^1/$_2$ fl oz)**
Dark chocolate	**80 g (3 oz), melted**

Prepare round Oreo Crust.

In a small saucepan, warm water and 55 g (2 oz) sugar over low heat until sugar has completely dissolved. Remove from heat and stir in green tea powder until smooth. Set aside to cool.

Preheat oven to 160°C (325°F).

With an electric mixer, beat cream cheese and remaining sugar at medium speed until creamy. Beat in vanilla essence and sifted corn flour until smooth.

Lower speed and add eggs, a little at a time, mixing until just incorporated. Gradually add whipping cream and milk until well mixed.

Divide filling into 2 equal portions. Blend melted dark chocolate into 1 portion and green tea mixture into the other.

Pour chocolate filling onto prepared crust. Bake in a water bath for 25–30 minutes. Remove from oven and carefully pour in green tea filling, taking care not to disturb chocolate layer.

Return cheesecake to oven and bake a further 45–55 minutes, or until edges of filling are set and centre is slightly wobbly. Turn off oven and leave cheesecake inside for 30 minutes with oven door closed. Prop open door and leave for another 30 minutes. Remove cheesecake from oven and cool on a wire rack.

Refrigerate for at least 6 hours before unmoulding. Decorate as desired before serving.

Makes an 18-cm (7-in) round cheesecake

Volcanoes

These moist chocolate cupcakes with creamy cheesecake centres are sure to be a hit with both children and adults. They are best served on the day they are made.

Cream Cheese Filling

Cream cheese	115 g (4 oz)
Castor (superfine) sugar	70 g (2¹/₂ oz)
Vanilla essence	¹/₄ tsp
Egg	¹/₂, large, lightly beaten

Fudgy Chocolate Cupcake Batter

Cake flour	100 g (3¹/₂ oz)
Cocoa powder	5³/₄ Tbsp
Baking powder	³/₄ tsp
Salt	¹/₃ tsp
Butter	100 g (3¹/₂ oz), softened
Castor (superfine) sugar	70 g (2¹/₂ oz)
Light brown sugar	70 g (2¹/₂ oz)
Vanilla essence	²/₃ tsp
Eggs	1¹/₂, large, lightly beaten
Milk	140 ml (4¹/₂ fl oz)

Prepare cream cheese filling. In a medium bowl, blend cream cheese, sugar and vanilla essence until smooth and creamy. Gradually add egg, beating until smooth. Set aside.

Preheat oven to 180°C (350°F). Line a 12-hole cupcake tin with paper cups.

Prepare cupcake batter. In a medium bowl, stir together cake flour, cocoa powder, baking powder and salt until well blended. Set aside.

With an electric mixer, cream butter, castor sugar and light brown sugar at medium speed until smooth and fluffy. Gradually blend in vanilla essence and eggs until well incorporated.

Lower speed and add flour mixture and milk in 3 separate additions, starting and ending with flour mixture. Make sure each addition is fully incorporated into batter before adding the next.

Divide batter evenly among paper cups. Create a cavity in the centre of each cupcake with the back of a spoon. Fill cavities with cream cheese filling.

Bake for 25–30 minutes, or until tops are lightly browned and spring back when gently pressed. Leave to cool in tin for 10 minutes.

Remove cupcakes from tin and leave to cool completely on a wire rack before serving. The cupcakes can be stored, covered, at room temperature for up to 3 days, or in the refrigerator for up to 1 week.

Makes 12 cupcakes

Chocolate Malt Cheesecake

Inspired by the classic chocolate malt shake found in old-fashioned American diners, we've managed to capture its goodness in the form of this sensational baked cheesecake.

18-cm (7-in) round Oreo Crust (see pg 146)	**1**
Milk	75 ml (2¹/₂ fl oz)
Chocolate malt powder (eg. Milo)	80 g (2³/₄ oz)
Cream cheese	450 g (16 oz)
Castor (superfine) sugar	60 g (2 oz)
Vanilla essence	¹/₃ tsp
Corn flour (cornstarch)	2¹/₃ Tbsp, sifted
Eggs	2, large
Whipping cream	75 ml (2¹/₂ fl oz)

Prepare round Oreo Crust.

In a small saucepan, warm milk over low heat until just about to boil. Remove from heat and stir in chocolate malt powder until completely dissolved. Set aside to cool.

Preheat oven to 160°C (325°F).

With an electric mixer, beat cream cheese and sugar at medium speed until creamy. Beat in vanilla essence and sifted corn flour until smooth.

Lower speed and add eggs, 1 at a time, mixing until just incorporated. Gradually add whipping cream and chocolate malt mixture until well mixed.

Pour filling onto prepared crust. Bake in a water bath for 1 hour 10 minutes–1 hour 30 minutes, or until edge of filling is set and centre is slightly wobbly.

Turn off oven and leave cheesecake inside for 30 minutes with oven door closed. Prop open door and leave for another 30 minutes. Remove cheesecake from oven and cool on a wire rack.

Refrigerate for at least 6 hours before unmoulding. Cut into wedges or squares and decorate as desired before serving.

Makes an 18-cm (7-in) round cheesecake

Chocolate Chip-Mocha Swirl Cheesecake

This robust and full-bodied cheesecake is kicked up a notch with the addition of chocolate chips. Use either dark or milk chocolate chips, whichever you prefer.

18-cm (7-in) round Oreo Crust (see pg 146)	1
Instant coffee granules	$^3/_4$ Tbsp
Hot water	$^3/_4$ Tbsp
Cream cheese	470 g (1 lb $^1/_2$ oz)
Light brown sugar	115 g (4 oz)
Vanilla essence	$^1/_3$ tsp
Corn flour (cornstarch)	2$^1/_2$ Tbsp, sifted
Eggs	2, large
Whipping cream	80 ml (2$^1/_2$ fl oz)
Milk	80 ml (2$^1/_2$ fl oz)
Dark chocolate	45 g (1$^1/_2$ oz), melted
Dark or milk chocolate chips	90 g (3$^1/_4$ oz)

Prepare round Oreo Crust.

In a small bowl, dissolve coffee granules in hot water. Set aside.

Preheat oven to 160°C (325°F).

With an electric mixer, beat cream cheese and light brown sugar at medium speed until creamy. Beat in vanilla essence, sifted corn flour and coffee mixture until smooth.

Lower speed and add eggs, 1 at a time, mixing until just incorporated. Gradually add whipping cream and milk until well mixed.

Divide filling into 2 equal portions. Blend melted chocolate into 1 portion and fold in the chocolate chips.

Pour plain coffee filling onto prepared crust. Spoon chocolate-coffee filling on top and using a spatula, create a marble-like effect by swirling the mixture lightly.

Bake in a water bath for 1 hour 10 minutes–1 hour 30 minutes, or until edge of filling is set and centre is slightly wobbly. Turn off oven and leave cheesecake inside for 30 minutes with oven door closed. Prop open door and leave for another 30 minutes. Remove cheesecake from oven and cool on a wire rack.

Refrigerate for at least 6 hours before unmoulding. Slice to serve.

Makes an 18-cm (7-in) round cheesecake

Milk Chocolate Cheesecake with Homemade Honey-roasted Cashew Nut Brittle

This cheesecake proves that milk chocolate can be as spectacular as dark chocolate when used in a baked cheesecake. If you fancy, substitute other nuts such as almonds or pistachios, for the brittle.

18-cm (7-in) round Oreo Crust (see pg 146)	**1**

Filling

Cream cheese	**450 g (1 lb)**
Castor (superfine) sugar	**75 g (2³/₄ oz)**
Vanilla essence	**¹/₃ tsp**
Corn flour (cornstarch)	**1³/₄ Tbsp, sifted**
Milk chocolate	**105 g (3³/₄ oz), melted**
Eggs	**2, large**
Whipping cream	**75 ml (2¹/₂ fl oz)**
Milk	**75 ml (2¹/₂ fl oz)**

Honey-roasted Cashew Nut Brittle

Castor (superfine) sugar	**150 g (5¹/₄ oz)**
Water	**3 Tbsp**
Honey-roasted cashew nuts	**30 g (1 oz), coarsely chopped**

Prepare round Oreo Crust.

Preheat oven to 160°C (325°F).

Prepare filling. With an electric mixer, beat cream cheese and sugar at medium speed until creamy. Beat in vanilla essence, sifted corn flour and melted milk chocolate until smooth.

Lower speed and add eggs, 1 at a time, mixing until just incorporated. Gradually add whipping cream and milk until well mixed.

Pour filling onto prepared crust. Bake in a water bath for 1 hour 10 minutes–1 hour 30 minutes, or until edge of filling is set and centre is slightly wobbly. Turn off oven and leave cheesecake inside for 30 minutes with oven door closed. Prop open door and leave for another 30 minutes.

Remove cheesecake from oven and cool on a wire rack. Refrigerate for at least 6 hours before unmoulding.

Prepare honey-roasted cashew nut brittle. In a medium saucepan, warm sugar and water over medium heat until sugar has completely dissolved.

Increase heat to high and bring mixture to the boil, stirring occasionally, until medium amber in colour. This takes 8–10 minutes.

Stir in chopped cashews. Working quickly and carefully, spread mixture evenly on an oiled baking sheet. Leave to cool before peeling off baking sheet and breaking brittle into pieces. Store at room temperature in an airtight container. Decorate cheesecake with brittle before serving.

Makes an 18-cm (7-in) round cheesecake

Gâteau Au Fromage Blanc De Forêt

A twist on the German classic, this white forest cheesecake features kirsch-soaked cherries and a chocolate sponge cake encased in a heavenly white chocolate cream cheese mousse. White rum works just as well in place of the kirsch.

18-cm (7-in) round Chocolate Sponge Cake (see pg 150)	**1, sliced horizontally into 2 layers**
Sugar Syrup (see pg 152)	

Macerated Pitted Dark Cherries

Drained pitted dark cherries in syrup	**85 g (3 oz), or about 12–14 whole cherries, halved and reserve 1 Tbsp syrup**
Kirsch or white rum	**1 Tbsp**

Filling

Gelatine powder	**1¹/₂ Tbsp**
Water	**55 ml (2 fl oz)**
Cream cheese	**265 g (9¹/₄ oz)**
Castor (superfine) sugar	**2 Tbsp**
White chocolate	**125 g (4¹/₂ oz), melted and still slightly warm**
Whipping cream	**105 ml (3¹/₂ fl oz)**
Milk	**105 ml (3¹/₂ fl oz)**
Kirsch or white rum	**1¹/₃ Tbsp**

Prepare round Chocolate Sponge Cake.

Prepare macerated cherries. Toss cherry halves, reserved syrup and kirsch or white rum in a small bowl. Cover and leave overnight in the refrigerator. Drain well before using.

Wrap the bottom of an 18-cm (7-in) round cake ring with aluminium foil and place on a baking tray. This will prevent the syrup or mousse from seeping out and creating a mess on the tray when assembling and chilling the cake.

Prepare filling. In a small saucepan, soak gelatine in water for 10 minutes. Warm over low heat until gelatine has dissolved. Leave to cool.

With an electric mixer, beat cream cheese and sugar at medium speed until creamy. Beat in melted white chocolate until smooth. Lower speed and gradually add whipping cream, milk, kirsch or white rum and gelatine mixture, mixing until well incorporated.

To assemble, place a layer of sponge into prepared cake ring and moisten with some sugar syrup. Pour one-third of filling into ring. Scatter in cherry halves and cover with another one-third of filling. Lightly press second layer of sponge on filling and moisten with remaining syrup. Pour in remaining filling.

Refrigerate cheesecake for at least 4 hours before unmoulding. Slice and decorate as desired before serving.

Makes an 18-cm (7-in) round cheesecake

Photo on previous page

Luscious Midnight Chocolate Tartlets

These rich and buttery chocolate tart shells carry a bittersweet chocolate-cream cheese filling similar to a firm-textured, baked chocolate ganache. To maintain its truffle-like consistency, take care not to overbake the tartlets.

Chocolate Sweet Crust Dough for six 7.5-cm (3-in) round tartlets (see pg 148)	**1 portion**
Filling	
Unsalted butter	**1^1/$_4$ Tbsp**
Warm water	**1^2/$_3$ Tbsp**
Dark chocolate	**70 g (2^1/$_2$ oz), finely chopped**
Cream cheese	**75 g (2^3/$_4$ oz)**
Castor (superfine) sugar	**2^1/$_2$ Tbsp**
Egg	**1, large, lightly beaten**
Chocolate Ganache	
Dark chocolate	**50 g (1^3/$_4$ oz), finely chopped**
Whipping cream	**3^1/$_3$ Tbsp**
Garnish (optional)	
Edible gold dust	
Icing (confectioner's) sugar	

Butter and flour six 7.5-cm (3-in) diameter tartlet pans.

Prepare Chocolate Sweet Crust Dough. On a floured surface, roll dough to about 0.5-cm (^{1}/$_4$-in) thick. Using an 11-cm (4^1/$_2$-in) cookie cutter, cut out 6 rounds. Transfer dough rounds to tartlet pans, lining the bottom and sides evenly. Trim off excess dough with a paring knife. Prick base all over with a fork and refrigerate shells for at least 1 hour before using.

Preheat oven to 160°C (325°F).

Prepare filling. In a small saucepan over medium heat, melt butter in warm water. Remove from heat and immediately stir in chopped chocolate until completely melted and smooth.

In a medium bowl, beat cream cheese and sugar until creamy. Gradually add egg and chocolate mixture, mixing until smooth.

Pour filling into chilled shells until about three-quarters full. Bake for 25–30 minutes, or until filling is risen and almost firm to the touch. Remove from oven and leave to cool in pans on a wire rack.

Prepare ganache. Place chopped chocolate in a small bowl. Bring cream to the boil. Pour over chopped chocolate and stir gently until smooth. Cool until ganache is just slightly warm.

Remove tartlets from pans and spread ganache on top. Refrigerate for 3 hours. Stand tartlets at room temperature for 10 minutes before serving. Dust with edible gold dust or icing sugar as desired.

Makes six 7.5-cm (3-in) round tartlets

White Chocolate and Strawberry Parfaits

White chocolate and the magnificent flavour of strawberries pair together perfectly. This alluring and visually stunning dessert is perfect for an after-meal treat.

Macerated Strawberries

Strawberries	**250 g (8³/₄ oz), diced**
Lemon juice	**1¹/₂ Tbsp**
Castor (superfine) sugar	**3 Tbsp**

White Chocolate-cream Cheese Mousse

Gelatine powder	**1 Tbsp**
Water	**2¹/₂ Tbsp**
Cream cheese	**225 g (8 oz)**
Castor (superfine) sugar	**1³/₄ Tbsp**
White chocolate	**105 g (3³/₄ oz), melted and still slightly warm**
Whipping cream	**6 Tbsp**
Milk	**6 Tbsp**

Prepare macerated strawberries. In a non-reactive bowl, toss together diced strawberries, lemon juice and sugar. Leave to stand for 10–15 minutes.

Prepare white chocolate-cream cheese mousse. In a small saucepan, soak gelatine in water for 10 minutes. Warm over low heat until gelatine is completely dissolved. Set aside.

With an electric mixer, beat cream cheese and sugar at medium speed until creamy. Beat in melted white chocolate and gelatine mixture until smooth. Lower speed and gradually add whipping cream and milk until well mixed.

To assemble, arrange 10–12 small glasses on a tray. Divide mousse into 3 portions and spoon 1 portion evenly into glasses. Divide half of the strawberries evenly among glasses and cover with another portion of mousse. Repeat to layer remaining strawberries and mousse. Refrigerate for 4 hours. Decorate as desired before serving.

Makes 10–12 small glasses

Marbled Chocolate Crème-Oreo Cheesecake

This updated variation of the classic Cookies 'n' Cream cheesecake uses chocolate-crème filled Oreo cookies instead of the traditional vanilla crème ones. We've made it doubly divine by infusing it with a dark chocolate cheesecake swirl.

18-cm (7-in) round Oreo Crust (see pg 146)	**1**
Cream cheese	**450 g (1 lb)**
Castor (superfine) sugar	**80 g (2³/₄ oz)**
Vanilla essence	**¹/₃ tsp**
Corn flour (cornstarch)	**2 Tbsp, sifted**
Eggs	**2, large**
Whipping cream	**75 ml (2¹/₂ fl oz)**
Milk	**75 ml (2¹/₂ fl oz)**
Dark chocolate	**45 g (1¹/₂ oz), melted**
Chocolate crème Oreo cookies	**60 g (2 oz), coarsely chopped**

Prepare round Oreo Crust.

Preheat oven to 160°C (325°F).

With an electric mixer, beat cream cheese and sugar at medium speed until creamy. Beat in vanilla essence and sifted corn flour until smooth.

Lower speed and add eggs, 1 at a time, mixing until just incorporated. Gradually add whipping cream and milk until well mixed.

Divide filling into 2 portions. Blend melted chocolate into 1 portion and fold chopped Oreo cookies into the other. Pour chocolate filling onto prepared crust. Spoon Oreo-cookie filling over and using a spatula, create a marble-like effect by swirling the mixture lightly.

Bake in a water bath for 1 hour 10 minutes–1 hour 30 minutes, or until edge of filling is set and centre is slightly wobbly. Turn off oven and leave cheesecake inside for 30 minutes with oven door closed. Prop open door and leave for another 30 minutes. Remove cheesecake from oven and cool on a wire rack.

Refrigerate for at least 6 hours before unmoulding. Slice as desired before serving.

Makes an 18-cm (7-in) round cheesecake

Chocolate-Almond Javas

This dessert may look challenging to prepare, but it really isn't. You may bake the chocolate almond discs the day before. Store them covered, at room temperature, to prevent them from drying out.

Chocolate Almond Discs

Ground almonds	**45 g (1^1/$_2$ oz)**
Icing (confectioner's) sugar	**55 g (2 oz)**
Cocoa powder	**2 Tbsp**
Salt	**a pinch**
Egg whites	**3, medium**
Castor (superfine) sugar	**1 Tbsp**

Chocolate Ganache

Dark chocolate	**40 g (1^1/$_2$ oz), chopped**
Whipping cream	**2 Tbsp**

Coffee-Cream Cheese Mousse

Gelatine powder	**1 tsp**
Water	**2^1/$_2$ tsp**
Instant coffee granules	**1^1/$_4$ tsp**
Hot water	**2 tsp**
Cream cheese	**135 g (4^3/$_4$ oz)**
Castor (superfine) sugar	**1^2/$_3$ Tbsp**
Light brown sugar	**1^2/$_3$ Tbsp**
Whipping cream	**80 ml (2^1/$_2$ fl oz)**

Preheat oven to 180°C (350°F). Line a baking tray with baking paper.

Prepare chocolate almond discs. Sift together ground almonds, icing sugar, cocoa powder and salt. In a separate, clean mixing bowl, whisk egg whites with an electric mixer at medium speed until foamy. Increase speed to high and gradually add sugar, whisking until firm and glossy peaks form. Gently fold in almond mixture.

Transfer batter to a piping bag fitted with a 1-cm (^{1}/$_2$-in) tip. Pipe 24 discs, each about 5-cm (2-in) in diameter and 2.5-cm (1-in) apart on prepared baking tray. Bake for 13–15 minutes. Leave to cool completely on baking tray before removing. Store covered at room temperature.

Prepare ganache. Place chopped chocolate in a small bowl. Boil cream and pour over chopped chocolate. Stir gently until smooth. Leave to cool before spreading on flat sides of 12 chocolate discs. Place discs on a plate with ganache side facing up. Refrigerate discs to set ganache.

Prepare coffee-cream cheese mousse. In a small saucepan, soak gelatine in 2^1/$_2$ tsp water for 10 minutes. Warm over low heat until gelatine has dissolved. Set aside. Dissolve instant coffee in 2 tsp hot water.

In a medium bowl, blend cream cheese, castor sugar and light brown sugar until smooth and creamy. Mix in coffee and gelatine mixture.

In a separate bowl, whisk whipping cream until medium peaks form. Fold gently into cream cheese mixture.

To assemble, spoon mousse into a piping bag fitted with a 1-cm (^{1}/$_2$-in) tip. Pipe mousse on ganache-coated side of chilled discs. Sandwich with remaining discs. Refrigerate for 3 hours before serving.

Makes 12 javas

White Chocolate-Passion Fruit Mousse Cheesecake

The tartness of the passion fruit goes well with the sweet and creamy white chocolate in this glorious and delightful chilled cheesecake.

23-cm (9-in) round Classic Digestive Crust (see pg 145)	**1**
Passion fruit coulis (optional)	

Filling

Gelatine powder	**2^1/$_4$ Tbsp**
Water	**75 ml (2^1/$_4$ fl oz)**
Cream cheese	**545 g (1 lb 3^1/$_4$ oz)**
Castor (superfine) sugar	**90 g (3^1/$_4$ oz)**
White chocolate	**220 g (7^3/$_4$ oz), melted and still slightly warm**
Passion fruit purée	**6 Tbsp**
Whipping cream	**325 ml**

Garnish (optional)

Passion fruit coulis

Prepare Classic Digestive Crust.

In a small saucepan, soak gelatine in water for 10 minutes. Warm over low heat until gelatine has dissolved. Set aside to cool.

With an electric mixer, beat cream cheese and sugar at medium speed until creamy. Gradually blend in melted white chocolate, passion fruit purée and gelatine mixture until smooth.

In a separate bowl, beat whipping cream until medium peaks form. Fold one-third of cream into cream cheese mixture to lighten. Gently fold in remaining cream until just incorporated.

Spread filling evenly over prepared crust and level top with a spatula. Refrigerate cheesecake for at least 6 hours before unmoulding.

Slice into wedges or rectangular pieces and drizzle with passion fruit coulis, if using. Decorate as desired before serving.

Makes a 23-cm (9-in) round cheesecake

Fruits

Apricot Almond-Cheese Tart

Our version of the classic almond cream tart uses a cream cheese-enriched filling. Slow-cooking, then steeping the apricots overnight makes them meltingly tender after the tart is baked.

Sweet Crust Dough
 for a 23-cm (9-in)
 round (see pg 148)   1 portion

Apricots

Castor (superfine) **sugar**	100 g (3¹/₂ oz)
Water	500 ml (16 fl oz / 2 cups)
Dried apricots	200 g (7 oz)

Cream Cheese-almond Filling

Butter	50 g (1³/₄ oz)
Cream cheese	100 g (3¹/₂ oz), softened
Icing (confectioner's) **sugar**	100 g (3¹/₂ oz)
Egg	1, large
Egg yolk	1, large
Vanilla essence	1 tsp
Ground almonds	90 g (3¹/₄ oz)

Note: Blind-baking is the process of baking an empty tart shell without its filling (in order to cook the shell partially). Weigh the shell down with rice, beans or pie weights so the pastry does not bubble up when baking.

Prepare apricots. In a saucepan, heat sugar and water over medium heat until sugar has dissolved. Add dried apricots and bring to the boil.

Lower heat and simmer for 25–30 minutes or until apricots have softened and syrup has reduced by half. Leave to cool then cover and stand for at least 6 hours. Drain well before using.

Prepare Sweet Crust Dough. Butter and flour a 23-cm (9-in) tart pan with a removable bottom. On a floured surface, roll dough to approximately 0.5-cm (¹/₄-in) thick. Transfer dough to pan, lining bottom and sides evenly. Trim off excess dough with a paring knife. Prick base all over with a fork and refrigerate for 1 hour.

Preheat oven to 175°C (350°F). Blind bake crust for 13–18 minutes or until surface is barely brown. Do not overbake. Remove from oven, then reduce oven temperature to 150°C (300°F).

Prepare filling. Beat butter, cream cheese and icing sugar until creamy. Gradually blend in egg, egg yolk and vanilla essence until smooth. Stir in ground almonds.

Spread filling on tart shell and arrange apricots evenly on top. Bake for 60–70 minutes, or until top is risen and lightly browned. Remove from oven and leave to cool on a wire rack.

Remove tart ring and transfer tart to a serving plate. Slice as desired and serve slightly warm or at room temperature.

Makes a 23-cm (9-in) round tart

Rhumba Mousse Cheesecake

The riper the bananas used, the sweeter and more aromatic this cheesecake will be. Keeping the bananas in a warm place can help speed up its ripening process.

23-cm (9-in) round Vanilla Sponge Cake (see pg 149)	**1, sliced horizontally into 2 layers**
Rum Syrup	
Sugar syrup (see pg 152)	**4 Tbsp**
White rum	**1 Tbsp**
Filling	
Gelatine powder	**2^1/$_4$ Tbsp**
Water	**75 ml (2^1/$_2$ fl oz)**
Peeled bananas	**250 g (8^3/$_4$ oz), very ripe and coarsely chopped**
Lemon juice	**1 Tbsp**
Cream cheese	**340 g (12 oz)**
Castor (superfine) sugar	**80 g (2^1/$_4$ oz)**
White rum	**2 Tbsp**
Whipping cream	**200 ml (6^2/$_3$ fl oz)**
Passion Fruit Gelée	
Gelatine powder	**1^1/$_4$ Tbsp**
Water	**240 ml (8 fl oz)**
Castor (superfine) sugar	**60 g (2 oz)**
Passion fruit purée	**50 g (1^3/$_4$ oz)**

Prepare round Vanilla Sponge Cake.

Wrap the base of a 23-cm (9-in) round cake ring that has a removable bottom with aluminium foil and place on a baking tray. This will prevent the syrup or mousse from seeping out and creating a mess on the tray when assembling and chilling the cake.

Prepare rum syrup. Stir together sugar syrup and white rum. Set aside.

Prepare filling. In a small saucepan, soak gelatine in water for 10 minutes. Warm over low heat until gelatine has dissolved. Leave to cool. In a blender (processor), purée bananas and lemon juice until smooth.

With an electric mixer, beat cream cheese and sugar at medium speed until creamy. Gradually add banana purée, white rum and gelatine mixture, mixing until smooth.

In a separate mixing bowl, beat whipping cream until medium-soft peaks form. Fold one-third of cream into cream cheese mixture to lighten. Gently fold in remaining cream until just incorporated.

To assemble, place a layer of sponge into prepared cake ring, moisten with some rum syrup, then pour in half the filling. Lightly press second layer of sponge on filling and moisten with more syrup. Pour in remaining filling. Refrigerate for 3 hours.

Prepare gelée. Soak gelatine in 40 ml (1^1/$_3$ fl oz) water in a small bowl for 10 minutes. In a small saucepan, heat sugar and remaining water until sugar has completely dissolved. Remove from heat and immediately stir in gelatine mixture and passion fruit purée. Leave to cool before pouring over cake. Refrigerate for at least another 2 hours before unmoulding and serving.

Makes a 23-cm (9-in) round cheesecake

Peaches 'n' Cream Cheesecake Ice Cream

To make a smooth ice cream, churn the custard in an electric ice cream machine. Make it even more tempting by topping it with ready-made fruit sauce and a generous sprinkling of toasted sliced almonds.

Cream cheese	**135 g (4³/₄ oz)**
Egg	**1, large, lightly beaten**
Milk	**270 ml (8²/₃ fl oz)**
Whipping cream	**270 ml (8²/₃ fl oz)**
Castor (superfine) sugar	**200 g (7 oz)**
Vanilla essence	**1 tsp**
Lemon juice	**2 Tbsp**
Digestive biscuits	**40 g (1¹/₂ oz), crumbled**
Drained canned peaches in syrup	**150 g (5¹/₄ oz), finely chopped**

In a medium bowl, whisk cream cheese until softened and smooth. Gradually whisk in egg until well incorporated.

In a medium saucepan, warm milk, whipping cream and sugar over medium heat until just about to boil. Slowly pour over cream cheese mixture, whisking constantly.

Return combined mixture to saucepan and cook over low heat for 5–8 minutes, stirring constantly, until mixture thickens slightly. Remove from heat. Stir in vanilla essence and lemon juice. Let stand for 10 minutes. Strain and refrigerate, covered, for at least 4 hours.

Pour mixture into an ice cream machine and churn according to manufacturer's directions.

Before freezing, fold in crumbled digestive biscuits and chopped peaches. Transfer ice cream into an airtight container and freeze for 6 hours or until firm. Serve as desired.

Makes 8–12 servings

Mango-Kalamansi Mousse Cheesecake

This tropical-inspired cheesecake is cool, refreshing and slightly tangy. For this exotic creation, you can use either kalamansi juice or lime juice.

18-cm (7-in) round Vanilla Sponge Cake (see pg 149)	1, sliced horizontally into 2 layers
Sugar syrup (see pg 152)	
Mango	1, medium, ripe but still firm, peeled and cut into 1-cm ($^1/_2$-in) cubes

Filling

Gelatine powder	$1^1/_4$ Tbsp
Water	3 Tbsp
Cream cheese	185 g ($6^1/_2$ oz)
Castor (superfine) sugar	45 g ($1^1/_2$ oz)
Kalamansi or lime juice	$1^3/_4$ Tbsp
Lime zest	1 tsp
Sweetened mango purée	165 g ($5^3/_4$ oz)
Whipping cream	110 ml ($2^2/_3$ fl oz)

Mango Glaze

Gelatine powder	$^1/_2$ Tbsp
Water	65 ml ($2^1/_6$ fl oz)
Sweetened mango purée	70 g ($2^1/_2$ oz)

Wrap the base of an 18-cm (7-in) round cake ring that has a removable bottom with aluminium foil and place on a baking tray. This will prevent the syrup or mousse from seeping out and creating a mess on the tray when assembling and chilling the cake.

Prepare filling. In a small saucepan, soak gelatine in water for 10 minutes. Warm over low heat until gelatine has dissolved. Leave to cool.

With an electric mixer, beat cream cheese and sugar at medium speed until creamy. Add kalamansi or lime juice, lime zest, mango purée and gelatine mixture, mixing until smooth.

In a separate mixing bowl, beat whipping cream until medium-soft peaks form. Fold one-third of cream into cream cheese mixture to lighten. Gently fold in remaining cream until just incorporated.

To assemble, place a layer of sponge into prepared cake ring and moisten with some sugar syrup. Pour one-third of filling into ring. Scatter in mango cubes and cover with another one-third of filling. Lightly press second layer of sponge on filling and moisten with syrup. Pour in remaining filling. Refrigerate for 2 hours.

Prepare mango glaze. In a small saucepan, soak gelatine in water for 10 minutes. Warm over low heat until gelatine has dissolved. Remove from heat and stir in mango purée. Cool and pour over chilled cake. Refrigerate for at least another 2 hours before unmoulding. Slice and decorate as desired before serving.

Makes an 18-cm (7-in) round cheesecake

Lychee Charlotte Cheesecake

This stunning and sophisticated-looking cheesecake is a perfect centrepiece for any special occasion. A hint of ginger complements the flavour of the sweet lychees.

Sponge Cake & Fingers for Charlottes

Eggs	**2, yolks and whites separated**
Castor (superfine) sugar	**60 g (2 oz)**
Vanilla essence	**$1/4$ tsp**
Butter	**$3/4$ Tbsp, melted and cooled**
Cake flour	**50 g ($1^3/4$ oz), sifted**
Sugar syrup (see pg 152)	

Prepare sponge fingers. Place 1 rack each on the upper third and lower third of oven. Preheat to 180°C (350°F). Line the bottom of an 18-cm (7-in) round cake pan and 23 x 33-cm (9 x 13-in) baking tray with baking paper.

In a small bowl, whisk egg yolks, 2 tsp sugar and vanilla essence until pale yellow and thickened.

In a separate, clean mixing bowl, whisk egg whites with an electric mixer at medium speed until foamy. Increase speed to high and gradually add remaining sugar. Whisk until firm and glossy peaks form. Fold one-third of whites into egg yolk mixture to lighten. Gently fold in remaining whites, followed by cake flour until just incorporated.

Transfer two-thirds of batter into a large piping bag fitted with a 1-cm ($1/2$-in) round tip. Working quickly, pipe 2 rows of fingers, each about 6-cm ($2^1/2$-in) in length, onto baking tray. Place tray on top rack of oven.

Fold melted butter into remaining batter and pour into round pan. Place on bottom rack of oven.

Bake fingers for 20–25 minutes and cake for 14–16 minutes. To ensure even browning, switch racks around after about 10 minutes of baking. Leave to cool.

Line an 18-cm (7-in) cake ring. Place on a serving platter. Trim long side of each row of sponge fingers to obtain a straight edge. Line inside of ring with trimmed fingers.

continued on next page

Filling

Canned lychees in syrup	1 can, 565 g (20 oz), well-drained
Gelatine powder	1 Tbsp
Water	2 Tbsp
Cream cheese	225 g (8 oz)
Castor (superfine) sugar	100 g (3^1/$_2$ oz)
Lemon juice	1^1/$_3$ tsp
Vanilla essence	^{2}/$_3$ tsp
Ground ginger	^{1}/$_3$ tsp
Whipping cream	130 ml (4 fl oz), chilled

Garnish (Optional)

Fresh strawberries, halved

Trim round sponge to 15-cm (6-in) in diameter and place in centre of cake ring, top side facing down. The sponge should fit snugly.

Prepare filling. Coarsely chop one-third of drained lychees and reserve remainder for garnish. In a small saucepan, soak gelatine in water for 10 minutes. Warm over low heat until gelatine has dissolved. Leave to cool.

With an electric mixer, beat cream cheese and sugar at medium speed until creamy. Add lemon juice, vanilla essence, ground ginger and gelatine mixture, mixing until smooth.

In a separate mixing bowl, beat whipping cream until medium peaks form. Fold one-third of cream into cream cheese mixture to lighten. Gently fold in remaining cream until just incorporated.

To assemble, moisten sponge base with sugar syrup. Pour half of filling into ring. Sprinkle in chopped lychees and cover with remaining filling. Refrigerate cheesecake for at least 4 hours before unmoulding. Garnish with remaining lychees and fresh strawberry halves, if desired.

Makes an 18-cm (7-in) round cheesecake

Chempedak Cheesecake

Chempedak is a tropical fruit well-loved for its fragrant, golden yellow flesh. If unavailable, jackfruit flesh can be used as a substitute. It will make the cheesecake slightly sweeter but it works just as well in this recipe. For optimum flavour, use fruit that is very ripe.

23-cm (9-in) round Classic Digestive Crust (see pg 145)	**1**
Chempedak Purée	
Chempedak or jackfruit flesh	**270 g (9^1/$_2$ oz)**
Water	**190 ml (6^1/$_3$ fl oz)**
Castor (superfine) sugar	**60 g (2 oz)**
Filling	
Cream cheese	**750 g (1^1/$_2$ lb 2^1/$_2$ oz)**
Castor (superfine) sugar	**70 g (2^1/$_2$ oz)**
Corn flour (cornstarch)	**5 Tbsp, sifted**
Eggs	**3^1/$_2$, large, lightly beaten**
Whipping cream	**160 ml (5 fl oz)**
Garnish (optional)	
Strips of chempedak or jackfruit flesh	

Prepare round Classic Digestive Crust.

Prepare purée. In a medium saucepan, cook chempedak or jackfruit flesh, water and sugar over medium heat until sugar has dissolved. Lower heat and simmer until flesh is soft and syrup has reduced and thickened. Leave to cool. Strain flesh and reserve 3 Tbsp syrup. Purée flesh and reserved syrup in a blender until smooth.

Preheat oven to 160°C (325°F).

Prepare filling. With an electric mixer, beat cream cheese and sugar at medium speed until creamy. Beat in sifted corn flour until smooth. Lower speed and add eggs, a little at a time, mixing until just incorporated. Gradually add whipping cream until well mixed. Fold in purée.

Pour filling onto prepared crust. Bake in a water bath for 1 hour 40 minutes–2 hours, or until edge of filling is set and centre is slightly wobbly. Turn off oven and leave cheesecake inside for 45 minutes with oven door closed. Prop open door and leave for another 45 minutes. Remove cheesecake and cool on a wire rack.

Refrigerate for at least 8 hours before unmoulding. Slice and decorate as desired with strips of chempedak or jackfruit flesh before serving.

Makes a 23-cm (9-in) round cheesecake

Raspberry Ribbon Cheesecake

Tangy, raspberry-infused ribbons of cheese weave through this deliciously beautiful cheesecake. To make a restaurant-style presentation, serve each slice on a bed of fruit coulis, topped with fresh raspberries and white chocolate shavings.

18-cm (7-in) round Classic Digestive Crust (see pg 145)	**1**
Filling	
Cream cheese	**450 g (16 oz)**
Castor (superfine) sugar	**100 g (3^1/$_2$ oz)**
Corn flour (cornstarch)	**3 Tbsp, sifted**
Eggs	**2, large**
Whipping cream	**75 ml (2^1/$_2$ fl oz)**
Milk	**75 ml (2^1/$_2$ fl oz)**
Raspberry purée	**190 g (6^3/$_4$ oz)**

Prepare round Classic Digestive Crust.

Preheat oven to 160°C (325°F).

Prepare filling. With an electric mixer, beat cream cheese and sugar at medium speed until creamy. Beat in sifted corn flour until smooth.

Lower speed and add eggs, 1 at a time, mixing until just incorporated. Gradually add whipping cream and milk until well mixed.

Divide filling into 2 equal portions. Blend raspberry purée into 1 portion. Pour plain filling onto prepared crust, then spoon raspberry filling on top. Using a spatula, swirl filling to create a marble-like effect.

Bake in a water bath for 1 hour 10 minutes–1 hour 30 minutes, or until edge of filling is set and centre is slightly wobbly. Turn off oven and leave cheesecake inside for 30 minutes with oven door closed. Prop open door and leave for another 30 minutes. Remove cheesecake from oven and cool on a wire rack.

Refrigerate for at least 6 hours before unmoulding. Decorate as desired before serving.

Makes an 18-cm (7-in) round cheesecake

Marsala-Pear Cheesecake

Poaching the pears in spices and Marsala, a fortified wine of Sicilian origin, gives them a sweet and smoky flavour. You may use a good-quality sweet red wine instead of the Marsala, although the flavour will not be the same.

23-cm (9-in) square **Chocolate Sheet Sponge Cake** (see pg 151)	1
Sugar syrup (see pg 152)	
Cocoa powder (optional)	for dusting

Poached Pears in Marsala Wine

Sweet Marsala wine	125 ml (4 fl oz / $^1/_2$ cup)
Castor (superfine) sugar	2 tsp
Ground cinnamon	$^1/_4$ tsp
Ground all-spice	$^1/_8$ tsp
Lemon zest	$^1/_2$ tsp
Canned pear halves	2, large

Filling

Gelatine powder	$1^1/_4$ Tbsp
Water	3 Tbsp
Cream cheese	200 g (7 oz)
Castor (superfine) sugar	90 g ($3^1/_4$ oz)
Sweet Marsala wine	2 Tbsp
Whipping cream	150 ml (5 fl oz), chilled

Garnish (optional)
Cocoa powder

Prepare square Chocolate Sheet Sponge Cake. Trim to get a 23 x 9-cm (9 x $3^1/_2$-in) strip and a 23 x 6-cm (9 x $2^1/_2$-in) strip. Reserve remaining sponge for another use.

Prepare poached pears. In a small saucepan, heat Marsala wine and sugar over medium-high heat until sugar has completely dissolved. Stir in cinnamon, all-spice and lemon zest and bring to the boil. Lower heat and add pear halves. Simmer for 15–20 minutes, turning pears over halfway through. Strain and cool. Cut pears into 1-cm ($^1/_2$-in) cubes. Set aside.

Prepare filling. In a small saucepan, soak gelatine in water for 10 minutes. Warm over low heat until gelatine has dissolved. Leave to cool.

With an electric mixer, beat cream cheese and sugar at medium speed until creamy. Gradually beat in Marsala wine and gelatine mixture until smooth.

In a separate mixing bowl, beat whipping cream until medium peaks form. Fold one-third of cream into cream cheese mixture to lighten. Gently fold in remaining cream until just incorporated.

To assemble, line a 23 x 10-cm (9 x 4-in) log mould with plastic wrap. Pour in filling until one-third full. Moisten smaller sponge strip with sugar syrup, invert and place on mousse.

Sprinkle in pear cubes and cover with remaining filling until approximately 1-cm ($^1/_2$-in) from top edge of mould.

Moisten second sponge strip, invert and gently press into filling until level with top edge. Cover tightly with plastic wrap. Refrigerate for at least 4 hours.

To unmould, run a thin-bladed knife along the sides of mould. Invert onto a serving platter and remove plastic wrap. Decorate as desired and dust with cocoa powder before serving, if using.

Makes a 23 x 10-cm (9 x 4-in) log cheesecake

Pêche Royale Trifle with Kirsch-soaked Cherries

The visual play of layers is what makes this trifle a party-stunner. Trifle is a traditional English dessert consisting of layers of cake, custard, liqueur and fruit. Our version features a rich and luxurious mascarpone crème. You can assemble the layers in smaller glasses and serve them as individual portions—they will be just as attractive.

Drained canned pitted dark cherries	**380 g (13^1/$_2$ oz), halved, reserve 75 ml (2^1/$_2$ fl oz) syrup**
Kirsch	**75 ml (2^1/$_2$ fl oz)**
Plain pound cake	**300 g (10^1/$_2$ oz), cut into 2.5-cm (1-in) cubes**
Drained canned peaches	**380 g (13^1/$_2$ oz), coarsely chopped**
Mascarpone Crème	
Mascarpone cheese	**270 g (9^1/$_2$ oz)**
Castor (superfine) sugar	**85 g (3 oz)**
Sour cream	**250 g (8^3/$_4$ oz)**
Whipping cream	**260 ml (8^1/$_3$ fl oz)**

Garnish (optional)
Drained canned peaches
Pitted dark cherries
Unsalted pistachio nuts
Toasted slivered almonds

In a medium bowl, toss drained cherry halves with reserved syrup and kirsch. Cover and allow to stand for 1 hour.

Prepare mascarpone crème. With an electric mixer, beat mascarpone cheese and sugar at medium speed until smooth. Blend in sour cream.

In a separate mixing bowl, beat whipping cream until medium-soft peaks form. Fold one-third of cream into mascarpone cheese mixture to lighten. Gently fold in remaining cream until just incorporated.

To assemble, line the bottom of a large trifle or glass bowl with two-thirds of pound cake cubes. Ensure cubes fit snugly with very few gaps in between. Cover with one-third of mascarpone crème. Spoon dark cherries and syrup over, followed by another third of crème. Cover with chopped peaches and spoon in remaining crème. Arrange remaining pound cake cubes on top.

Cover and refrigerate for at least 12 hours. Before serving, decorate top of trifle with drained canned peaches, pitted dark cherries, unsalted pistachio nuts and toasted slivered almonds, if desired.

Serves 12–16

Caribbean Cheesecake

The pineapple flesh releases juicy bits of flavour when you bite into this delectable tropical cheesecake.

23-cm (9-in) round **Classic Digestive** **Crust (see pg 145)**	**1**

Filling

Drained canned **pineapple**	**465 g (1 lb ¹/₂ oz)**
Cream cheese	**750 g (1¹/₂ lb 2¹/₂ oz)**
Light brown sugar	**120 g (4¹/₄ oz)**
Corn flour (cornstarch)	**4¹/₄ Tbsp, sifted**
Rum essence	**2 tsp**
Eggs	**3¹/₂, lightly beaten**
Whipping cream	**160 ml (5 fl oz)**

Prepare round Classic Digestive Crust.

In a blender (processor), purée drained canned pineapple until smooth. Set aside.

Preheat oven to 160°C (325°F).

With an electric mixer, beat cream cheese and light brown sugar at medium speed until creamy. Beat in sifted corn flour and rum essence until smooth.

Lower speed and add eggs, a little at a time, mixing until just incorporated. Gradually add whipping cream until well mixed. Fold in puréed pineapple.

Pour filling onto prepared crust. Bake in a water bath for 1 hour 40 minutes–2 hours, or until edge of filling is set and centre is slightly wobbly. Turn off oven and leave cheesecake inside for 45 minutes with oven door closed. Prop open door and leave for another 45 minutes. Remove cheesecake from oven and cool on a wire rack.

Refrigerate for at least 8 hours before unmoulding. Slice and decorate as desired before serving.

Makes a 23-cm (9-in) round cheesecake

Heavenly Lemon Cloud Cheesecake

Incorporating whipped egg whites into the filling gives this tart and refreshing cheesecake a slightly crumbly but light texture.

23-cm (9-in) round Classic Digestive Crust (see pg 145)	**1**
Cream cheese	**550 g (1 lb 3^1/$_2$ oz)**
Castor (superfine) sugar	**210 g (7^1/$_2$ oz)**
Lemon juice	**65 ml (2^1/$_6$ fl oz)**
Lemon zest	**^{3}/$_4$ Tbsp**
Plain (all-purpose) flour	**4^1/$_3$ Tbsp, sifted**
Egg yolks	**3, large**
Egg whites	**4, large**

Garnish (optional)
Icing (confectioner's) sugar

Ground cinnamon

Lemon zest

Prepare round Classic Digestive Crust.

Preheat oven to 160°C (325°F).

With an electric mixer, beat cream cheese and 170 g (6 oz) sugar at medium speed until creamy.

Beat in lemon juice, lemon zest and sifted flour until smooth. Lower speed and add egg yolks, 1 at a time, mixing until just incorporated.

In a separate, clean mixing bowl, whisk egg whites with an electric mixer at medium speed until foamy. Increase speed to high and gradually add remaining sugar. Whisk until firm and glossy peaks form.

Fold one-third of egg whites into cheese mixture to lighten. Gently fold in remaining egg whites until just incorporated.

Pour filling onto prepared crust. Bake for 1 hour 10 minutes– 1 hour 30 minutes, or until filling is set and top is lightly browned. Remove from oven and cool on a wire rack.

Refrigerate for at least 6 hours before unmoulding and serving.

Makes a 23-cm (9-in) round cheesecake

Orange Cream Cheese and Cranberry Turnovers

A flaky crust enriched with cream cheese encases a tangy, creamy filling paired with tart cranberries. Great as a breakfast treat or an afternoon tea snack.

Cream Cheese Dough

Butter	**110 g (4 oz), softened**
Cream cheese	**150 g (5^1/$_4$ oz)**
Plain (all-purpose) flour	**190 g (6^3/$_4$ oz)**

Filling

Dried cranberries	**35 g (1^1/$_4$ oz)**
Freshly squeezed orange juice	**2 Tbsp**
Cream cheese	**85 g (3 oz)**
Castor (superfine) sugar	**2^3/$_4$ Tbsp**
Egg	**1, large, yolk and white separated**
Plain (all-purpose) flour	**1 tsp**
Orange zest	**^{1}/$_2$ tsp**

Prepare cream cheese dough. With an electric mixer, beat butter and cream cheese at medium speed until smooth. Lower speed and add flour, mixing until dough just comes together. Divide dough into 2 equal balls and cover each ball with plastic wrap. Refrigerate for at least 1 hour.

Prepare filling. In a small saucepan, cook dried cranberries and orange juice over medium heat until cranberries are plump and juice has reduced by two-thirds. Remove from heat and set aside.

In a medium bowl, blend cream cheese and sugar until creamy. Beat in egg yolk, flour and orange zest until smooth.

Preheat oven to 185°C (350°F). Lightly grease a large baking tray with butter or vegetable shortening.

Work with 1 ball of dough at a time. Unwrap dough and roll it on a floured surface to 0.25-cm (^{1}/$_8$-in) thick. Cut out 6 rounds with a 9-cm (3^1/$_2$-in) round cookie cutter.

Place 2 tsp filling and 1 tsp cranberries in the centre of each round. Brush edges with beaten egg white and fold in half. Press edges to seal then crimp with a fork. Carefully transfer to greased baking tray.

Repeat with other ball of dough to make 12 turnovers in total.

Brush tops of turnovers with beaten egg white. Prick tops with a fork to allow turnovers to cook more evenly. Bake for 20–25 minutes, or until light golden brown.

Remove from oven and leave to cool for 10 minutes before serving. Serve warm or at room temperature.

Makes 12 turnovers

Mango Mousse Cheesecake with Strawberries in Red Gelée

These beautiful and dramatic mini cheesecakes are intensely sweet and flavourful. For a variation to this recipe, try substituting kiwis for strawberries and tint the gelée green.

23-cm (9-in) round Vanilla Sponge Cake (see pg 149)	**1, sliced horizontally into 2 layers**

Filling

Gelatine powder	**1 Tbsp**
Water	**2 Tbsp**
Cream cheese	**145 g (5 oz)**
Castor (superfine) sugar	**2³/₄ Tbsp**
Lemon juice	**1²/₃ tsp**
Sweetened mango purée	**135 g (4³/₄ oz)**
Whipping cream	**6 Tbsp, chilled**

Strawberries in Red Gelée Layer

Gelatine powder	**¹/₂ Tbsp**
Water	**3¹/₃ Tbsp**
Castor (superfine) sugar	**1¹/₄ Tbsp**
Red food colouring	**a few drops**
Whole strawberries	**6–8, large, hulled and coarsely chopped**

Prepare round Vanilla Sponge Cake. From 1 sponge layer, cut out 6 rounds using a 6-cm (2¹/₂-in) round cookie cutter. Reserve other layer for another use.

Prepare filling. In a small saucepan, soak gelatine in water for 10 minutes. Warm over low heat until gelatine has dissolved. Leave to cool.

With an electric mixer, beat cream cheese and sugar at medium speed until creamy. Add lemon juice, mango purée and gelatine mixture, mixing until smooth.

In a separate mixing bowl, beat whipping cream until medium peaks form. Fold one-third of cream into cream cheese mixture to lighten. Gently fold in remaining cream until just incorporated.

To assemble, wrap the base of six 7.5-cm (3-in) round cake rings with aluminium foil and place on a baking tray. This will prevent the syrup or mousse from seeping out and creating a mess on the tray when assembling and chilling the cakes.

Place a sponge round in the middle of each ring and divide filling evenly among rings. Press filling down with the back of a spoon. Refrigerate for 2 hours.

Prepare red gelée. Soak gelatine in 1 Tbsp water for 10 minutes. In a small saucepan, heat sugar and remaining water until sugar has completely dissolved. Remove from heat and stir in gelatine mixture until completely melted. When cool, tint with red food colouring.

Pour gelée over partially set filling and evenly distribute chopped strawberries among rings. Refrigerate for another 2 hours before unmoulding and serving.

Makes six 7.5-cm (3-in) round mini cheesecakes

Durian Crème Cheesecake

Hailed as "the king of fruit" in Southeast Asia, durians are fascinating as some love the aroma of its luxurious and custard-like flesh, whereas others find it overwhelming. For durian lovers, this cheesecake is an absolute must!

23-cm (9-in) round Vanilla Sponge Cake (see pg 149)	**1, sliced horizontally into 2 layers**
Sugar syrup (see pg 152)	

Filling

Gelatine powder	$2^1/_4$ Tbsp
Water	80 ml ($2^2/_3$ fl oz)
Durian flesh	220 g ($7^3/_4$ oz)
Salt	$^1/_4$ tsp
Eggs	2, large
Castor (superfine) sugar	110 g (4 oz)
Cream cheese	360 g ($12^3/_4$ oz)
Whipping cream	240 ml (8 fl oz)

Garnish (optional)

Lightly toasted pine nuts

Note: As durian flesh spoils within a few days and its aroma spreads easily, store cheesecake tightly covered in the refrigerator and consume within 3 days.

Prepare round Vanilla Sponge Cake.

Wrap the base of a 23-cm (9-in) round cake ring that has a removable bottom with aluminium foil and place on a baking tray. This will prevent the syrup or mousse from seeping out and creating a mess on the tray when assembling and chilling the cake.

Prepare filling. In a small saucepan, soak gelatine in water for 10 minutes. Warm over low heat until gelatine has dissolved. Leave to cool.

Purée durian flesh with salt in a blender until smooth. Set aside.

Place eggs and 1 Tbsp sugar in a heatproof mixing bowl and set over a pot of simmering water. Whisk until pale and thickened. Remove from heat. Immediately stir in gelatine mixture and durian purée.

With an electric mixer, beat cream cheese and remaining sugar at medium speed until creamy. Lower speed and gradually add durian mixture, mixing until smooth.

In a separate mixing bowl, beat whipping cream until medium peaks form. Fold one-third of cream into cream cheese mixture to lighten. Gently fold in remaining whipped cream until just incorporated.

To assemble, place one layer of sponge into prepared cake ring and moisten with some syrup. Pour half of filling into ring. Lightly press second layer of sponge on filling and moisten with more syrup. Pour in remaining filling. Refrigerate for at least 4 hours before unmoulding.

Slice and garnish as desired with toasted pine nuts before serving.

Makes a 23-cm (9-in) round cheesecake

Summer Berry Tiramisu

This luscious cheesecake filled with sweet, juicy berries is simply brimming with the goodness of summer. Use one or any combination of berries suggested in the recipe.

18-cm (7-in) round Vanilla Sponge Cake (see pg 149)	**1, sliced horizontally into 2 layers**
Kirsch Syrup	
Sugar syrup (see pg 152)	**4 Tbsp**
Kirsch	**1 Tbsp**
Filling	
Mixed berries (strawberries, blackberries, blueberries and/or raspberries)	**100 g (3¹/₂ oz)**
Castor (superfine) sugar	**80 g (3 oz)**
Lemon juice	**1 tsp**
Gelatine powder	**1 Tbsp**
Water	**2 Tbsp**
Egg yolks	**4, large**
Kirsch	**2 Tbsp**
Cream cheese	**135 g (4³/₄ oz), softened**
Whipping cream	**155 ml (5 fl oz)**
Garnish (optional)	
Mixed berries (strawberries, blueberries, raspberries, blackberries)	

Prepare round Vanilla Sponge Cake.

Wrap the base of an 18-cm (7-in) round cake ring that has a removable bottom with aluminium foil and place on a baking tray. This will prevent the syrup or mousse from seeping out and creating a mess on the tray when assembling and chilling the cake.

Prepare kirsch syrup. Stir together syrup and kirsch. Set aside.

Prepare filling. In a non-reactive bowl, toss together berries, 25 g (1 oz) sugar and lemon juice. Leave to stand for 30 minutes. Drain berries well.

In a small saucepan, soak gelatine in water for 10 minutes. Warm over low heat until gelatine has dissolved. Leave to cool.

Place egg yolks and remaining sugar in a heatproof mixing bowl and set over a pot of simmering water. Whisk until yolks become pale and glossy. Remove from heat. Stir in gelatine mixture and kirsch. Gradually blend egg yolk mixture into softened cream cheese until smooth.

In a separate mixing bowl, beat whipping cream until medium-soft peaks form. Fold one-third of cream into cream cheese mixture to lighten. Gently fold in remaining cream until just incorporated.

To assemble, place a layer of sponge cake into prepared cake ring and moisten with half of kirsch syrup. Pour one-third of filling into ring. Sprinkle in berries and cover with another one-third of filling. Lightly press second layer of sponge on filling and moisten with remaining syrup. Pour in remaining filling. Refrigerate for at least 4 hours before unmoulding and serving. Garnish with mixed berries, if desired.

Makes an 18-cm (7-in) round cheesecake

Strawberry-Balsamic Vinegar Cheesecake

Pairing strawberries with balsamic vinegar may be unconventional, but don't worry—the combination works out surprisingly well. The vinegar enhances the sweetness and fragrance of the strawberries.

18-cm (7-in) round **Classic Digestive** **Crust (see pg 145)**	**1**

Balsamic Vinegar Strawberries

Castor (superfine) **sugar**	**50 g (1^3/$_4$ oz)**
Balsamic vinegar	**2^1/$_3$ Tbsp**
Strawberries	**250 g (8^3/$_4$ oz), hulled and diced**

Filling

Cream cheese	**450 g (16 oz)**
Castor (superfine) **sugar**	**100 g (3^1/$_2$ oz)**
Corn flour (cornstarch)	**2^1/$_4$ Tbsp, sifted**
Lemon juice	**2 tsp**
Eggs	**2, large**
Whipping cream	**75 ml (2^1/$_2$ oz)**
Milk	**75 ml (2^1/$_2$ oz)**

Garnish (optional)
Fresh whipped cream

Prepare round Classic Digestive Crust.

Prepare balsamic strawberries. In a large bowl, stir sugar in balsamic vinegar until dissolved. Toss in diced strawberries and let stand for 1 hour. Drain and reserve syrup. Reserve half of strawberries for garnish and discard the rest.

Preheat oven to 160°C (325°F).

Prepare filling. With an electric mixer, beat cream cheese and sugar at medium speed until creamy. Beat in sifted corn flour and lemon juice until smooth. Lower speed and add eggs, 1 at a time, mixing until just incorporated. Gradually add whipping cream and milk until well mixed.

Pour one-third of filling onto prepared crust and sprinkle in half the strawberries. Repeat. Pour in remaining filling, covering strawberries completely.

Bake in a water bath for 1 hour 10 minutes–1 hour 30 minutes, or until edge of filling is set and centre is slightly wobbly. Turn off oven and leave cheesecake inside for 30 minutes with oven door closed. Prop open door and leave for another 30 minutes. Remove cheesecake from oven and cool on a wire rack. Refrigerate for at least 6 hours before serving.

Prepare balsamic vinegar sauce. In a small saucepan, bring reserved syrup to the boil. Reduce heat to medium and simmer until slightly thickened or reduced by half. Leave sauce to cool.

Slice cheesecake as desired and drizzle cooled syrup over. Decorate with reserved balsamic strawberries and fresh whipped cream, if desired, before serving.

Makes an 18-cm (7-in) round cheesecake

Nuts about Candy

White Chocolate-Menthe Cheesecake

White chocolate and mint are quintessentially Christmas flavours, but whip this cheesecake up anytime of the year and it'll be a hit. The chopped chocolate-mint candies add an extra crunch to the cheesecake.

Oreo Crust

Oreo sandwich cookies	**130 g ($4^1/_2$ oz)**

Filling

Cream cheese	**570 g (1 lb 4 oz)**
Castor (superfine) sugar	**90 g ($2^1/_2$ oz)**
Corn flour (cornstarch)	**2 Tbsp, sifted**
Mint essence	**$1^1/_2$ tsp**
White chocolate	**140 g (5 oz), melted**
Eggs	**$2^1/_2$, large, lightly beaten**
Whipping cream	**95 ml ($3^1/_6$ fl oz)**
Milk	**95 ml ($3^1/_6$ fl oz)**
Chocolate-mint candy (eg. Andes)	**100 g ($3^1/_2$ oz), coarsely chopped**

Ganache Icing

Gelatine powder	**1 Tbsp**
Water	**2 Tbsp**
Whipping cream	**75 ml ($2^1/_2$ fl oz)**
Castor (superfine) sugar	**45 g ($1^1/_2$ oz)**
Dark chocolate	**190 g ($6^3/_4$ oz), finely chopped**

Prepare crust. Wrap the base of an 18-cm (7-in) square pan that has a removable bottom with a layer of aluminium foil. Place on a baking tray and set aside.

Break cookies into large chunks. Place in a blender (processor) and pulse until finely ground. Transfer ground cookies to prepared pan. With your hands (you may wish to wear disposable gloves), press ground cookies firmly into an even layer onto the bottom of pan. Refrigerate for at least 1 hour before using.

Preheat oven to 160°C (325°F).

Prepare filling. With an electric mixer, beat cream cheese and sugar at medium speed until creamy. Beat in sifted corn flour, mint essence and melted white chocolate until smooth.

Lower speed and add eggs, a little at a time, mixing until just incorporated. Gradually add whipping cream and milk until well mixed. Fold in chopped candy.

Pour filling onto prepared crust. Bake in a water bath for 1 hour 20 minutes–1 hour 40 minutes, or until edge of filling is set and centre is slightly wobbly. Turn off oven and leave cheesecake inside for 30 minutes with oven door closed. Prop open door and leave for another 30 minutes. Remove cheesecake from oven and cool on a wire rack. Refrigerate for at least 6 hours before unmoulding.

Prepare ganache icing. In a small saucepan, soak gelatine in water for 10 minutes. Warm over low heat until gelatine has dissolved. Leave to cool.

In a separate saucepan, heat cream and sugar over medium heat until boiling. Remove from heat and immediately stir in chopped chocolate until completely melted and mixture is smooth. Gradually blend in gelatine mixture. Cool until slightly warm before glazing top and sides of chilled cheesecake with a spatula.

Slice and decorate as desired before serving.

Makes an 18-cm (7-in) square cheesecake

Elvis Cheesecake Pops

Re-live your childhood memories with these peanut butter and brownie cheesecake pops dunked in dark chocolate. To make the pops, you will need disposable wooden ice cream sticks and a large styrofoam block.

Brownie Batter

Plain (all-purpose) flour	**105 g (3^3/$_4$ oz)**
Salt	**^{1}/$_4$ tsp**
Butter	**60 g (2 oz)**
Dark chocolate	**105 g (3^3/$_4$ oz), chopped**
Castor (superfine) sugar	**70 g (2^1/$_2$ oz)**
Light brown sugar	**75 g (2^3/$_4$ oz)**
Vanilla essence	**1^1/$_3$ tsp**
Eggs	**2, large**

Peanut Butter Cheese Filling

Cream cheese at room temperature	**225 g (8 oz)**
Light brown sugar	**50 g (1^3/$_4$ oz)**
Creamy peanut butter	**90 g (3^1/$_4$ oz)**
Egg	**1, large, lightly beaten**
Whipping cream	**70 ml (2^1/$_3$ fl oz)**

Chocolate Coating

Dark chocolate	**255 g (9 oz), chopped**
Vegetable shortening	**3 Tbsp (1^1/$_4$ oz)**
Banana essence	**1 tsp**
Toasted crushed almond slivers (optional)	**for coating**

Line bottom and sides of an 18-cm (7-in) square pan with aluminium foil, creating an overhang on each side. Butter and flour base of foil.

Prepare brownie batter. In a medium bowl, stir flour and salt together and set aside. Place butter and chopped chocolate in a heatproof bowl and set over a pot of simmering water. Stir until both are completely melted and smooth. Remove from heat. Stir in castor sugar, light brown sugar, vanilla essence and eggs. Fold in flour mixture until just moistened. Set aside while preparing filling.

Preheat oven to 175°C (350°F).

Prepare filling. With an electric mixer, beat cream cheese and brown sugar at medium speed until creamy. Blend in peanut butter until smooth. Lower speed and gradually add egg and whipping cream until well mixed.

Pour half of brownie batter into prepared pan, then pour peanut butter filling evenly over. Spoon remaining brownie batter over filling and, using a spatula, swirl to create a marbling effect.

Bake for 35–40 minutes, or until a toothpick inserted into the centre comes out with moist crumbs attached. Remove from oven and leave to cool in pan on a wire rack. Using foil extensions as handles, remove brownie from pan. Cut into squares. Insert an ice cream stick into each square. Refrigerate for 1 hour.

Make chocolate coating. Melt chocolate and shortening over a pot of simmering water then stir in banana essence. Leave to cool until slightly warm.

Dip squares into chocolate, letting excess drip off. Sprinkle toasted crushed almonds over to coat brownie squares, if desired.

Pierce ice cream sticks into a styrofoam block and refrigerate for 30 minutes to firm coating before serving. Store refrigerated.

Makes about 25 squares

Snickers Cheesecake

Nosh on this satisfying cheesecake embedded with chewy chunks of Snickers candy bar, a rich and gooey confection made from milk chocolate, caramel and peanuts.

23-cm (9-in) round Oreo Crust (see pg 146)	**1**
Snickers candy bars	**3, total 170 g (6 oz)**
Filling	
Cream cheese	**750 g (1 lb 10^1/$_2$ oz)**
Light brown sugar	**165 g (5^3/$_4$ oz)**
Corn flour (cornstarch)	**4 Tbsp, sifted**
Vanilla essence	**^{1}/$_2$ tsp**
Eggs	**4, medium**
Whipping cream	**120 ml (4 fl oz)**
Milk	**120 ml (4 fl oz)**

Prepare round Oreo Crust.

With a sharp knife, chop Snickers bars into 1-cm (^{1}/$_2$-in) chunks. Set aside.

Preheat oven to 160°C (325°F).

Prepare filling. With an electric mixer, beat cream cheese and light brown sugar at medium speed until creamy. Beat in sifted corn flour and vanilla essence until smooth.

Lower speed and add eggs, 1 at a time, mixing until just incorporated. Gradually add whipping cream and milk until well mixed.

Pour filling onto prepared crust. Sprinkle chopped Snickers evenly on top of filling. Bake in a water bath for 1 hour 40 minutes–2 hours, or until edge of filling is set and centre is slightly wobbly.

Turn off oven and leave cheesecake inside for 45 minutes with oven door closed. Prop open door and leave for another 45 minutes. Remove cheesecake from oven and cool on a wire rack.

Refrigerate for at least 8 hours before unmoulding and serving.

Makes a 23-cm (9-in) round cheesecake

Toasted Hazelnut Cheesecake

If you love nuts, this cheesecake is for you. Toasting the hazelnuts beforehand releases its superb flavour and aroma.

18-cm (7-in) round Classic Digestive Crust (see pg 145)	**1**
Blanched whole hazelnuts	**70 g (2^1/$_2$ oz)**
Cream cheese	**450 g (16 oz)**
Castor (superfine) sugar	**110 g (4 oz)**
Vanilla essence	**^{1}/$_3$ tsp**
Corn flour (cornstarch)	**1^3/$_4$ Tbsp, sifted**
Eggs	**2, large**
Whipping cream	**75 ml (2^1/$_2$ oz)**
Milk	**75 ml (2^1/$_2$ oz)**

Prepare round Classic Digestive Crust.

Spread hazelnuts on a baking tray. Toast in a preheated oven at 190°C (370°F) for 5–8 minutes, or until nuts are oily and lightly browned on the surface. Immediately transfer hot nuts to a blender (processor) and pulse until finely ground. Leave to cool.

Preheat oven to 160°C (325°F).

Prepare filling. With an electric mixer, beat cream cheese and sugar at medium speed until creamy. Beat in vanilla essence and sifted corn flour until smooth.

Lower speed and add eggs, 1 at a time, mixing until just incorporated. Gradually add whipping cream and milk until well mixed. Fold in cooled, ground hazelnuts.

Pour filling onto prepared crust. Bake in a water bath for 1 hour 10 minutes–1 hour 30 minutes, or until edge of filling is set and centre is slightly wobbly. Turn off oven and leave cheesecake inside for 30 minutes with oven door closed. Prop open door and leave for another 30 minutes. Remove cheesecake from oven and cool on a wire rack.

Refrigerate for at least 6 hours before unmoulding. Cut and decorate as desired to serve.

Makes an 18-cm (7-in) round cheesecake

Rocky Road-Caramel Cheesecake Tart

Candy lovers beware—this confection is extremely addictive. To emulate the classic rocky road flavour, use chopped peanuts for the garnish.

Chocolate Sweet Crust Dough for a 23-cm (9-in) round tart (see pg 148) — 1 portion

Caramel

Castor (superfine) sugar	120 g (4^1/$_4$ oz)
Water	2^1/$_3$ Tbsp
Whipping cream	70 ml (2^1/$_3$ fl oz)

Filling

Cream cheese	275 g (9^3/$_4$ oz)
Light brown sugar	1^2/$_3$ Tbsp
Vanilla essence	1 tsp
Salt	a pinch
Egg	1, large
Egg yolk	1, large

Garnish (optional)

Sweetened whipped cream (see pg 152)

Mini marshmallows

Toasted chopped nuts

Chocolate fudge sauce

Prepare Chocolate Sweet Crust Dough. Butter and flour a tart pan that has a removable bottom. On a floured surface, roll dough to approximately 0.5-cm (^{1}/$_4$-in) thick. Transfer dough to pan, lining bottom and sides evenly. Trim off excess dough with a paring knife and reserve for another use. Prick base all over with a fork, then refrigerate for at least 1 hour before using.

Prepare caramel. In a medium saucepan, warm sugar and water over medium heat until sugar has completely dissolved. Increase heat to high and boil mixture, stirring occasionally, until amber in colour, about 3–5 minutes. Slowly and carefully pour in cream. Lower heat and stir constantly until well-mixed. Remove from heat and let stand for 10 minutes. Caramel should be of a thick pouring consistency.

Preheat oven to 180°C (350°F).

Prepare filling. With an electric mixer, beat cream cheese, light brown sugar, vanilla essence and salt at medium speed until creamy. Lower speed and gradually add egg and egg yolk, mixing until just incorporated.

Fold in warm caramel until smooth. (If caramel becomes too firm, warm over very low heat to return it to pouring consistency. Do not overheat.)

Pour filling into chilled tart shell. Bake for 35–40 minutes, or until filling is risen, firm and golden brown. Remove from oven and cool on a wire rack.

Remove tart ring and transfer tart to a serving plate. Refrigerate for at least 3 hours. Just before serving, pipe sweetened whipped cream on top of tart and garnish with mini marshmallows, toasted chopped nuts and a generous drizzling of chocolate fudge sauce.

Makes an 18-cm (7-in) round tart

M&M's Celebration Cheesecake

Kids won't be able to resist this whimsical treat! The trimmings are as fun and delicious to eat as the cheesecake itself! Decorate with plain, peanut or almond M&M's candies, or let the kids exercise their creativity by involving them in the decorating process!

23-cm (9-in) round Oreo Crust (see pg 146)	**1**
Filling	
Cream cheese	**825 g (1^3/$_4$ lb 1 oz)**
Castor (superfine) sugar	**155 g (5^1/$_2$ oz)**
Corn flour (cornstarch)	**5 Tbsp, sifted**
Vanilla essence	**^{1}/$_2$ tsp**
Lemon juice	**2 tsp**
Eggs	**4, large**
Whipping cream	**130 ml (4^1/$_6$ fl oz)**
Milk	**130 ml (4^1/$_6$ fl oz)**
Topping	
Dark chocolate	**80 g (2^3/$_4$ oz), finely chopped**
Whipping cream	**100 ml (3^1/$_3$ fl oz)**
M&M's plain chocolate candies	**100 g (3^1/$_2$ oz)**

Prepare round Oreo Crust.

Preheat oven to 160°C (325°F).

Prepare filling. With an electric mixer, beat cream cheese and sugar at medium speed until creamy. Beat in sifted corn flour, vanilla essence and lemon juice until smooth.

Lower speed and add eggs, 1 at a time, mixing until just incorporated. Gradually add whipping cream and milk until well mixed.

Pour filling onto prepared crust. Bake in a water bath for 1 hour 40 minutes–2 hours, or until edge of filling is set and centre is slightly wobbly. Turn off oven and leave cheesecake inside for 45 minutes with oven door closed. Prop open door and leave for another 45 minutes. Remove cheesecake from oven and cool on a wire rack.

Prepare topping. Place chopped chocolate in a small bowl. Boil cream and pour over chopped chocolate. Let stand for 1 minute, then stir gently until smooth. When cool, spread topping evenly on top of cheesecake with a spatula.

Refrigerate for at least 8 hours before unmoulding. Slice and decorate as desired.

Makes a 23-cm (9-in) round cheesecake

Chocolate Chip-Banana Cheesecake on Walnut Crust

Put moist, caramelised bananas and crunchy chocolate chips in a creamy cheesecake on a fragrant walnut crust, and the final outcome is simply divine.

18-cm (7-in) round Classic Digestive Crust with walnuts (see pg 145)	**1**
Caramelised Bananas	
Butter	**1 Tbsp**
Castor (superfine) sugar	**45 g (1¹/₂ oz)**
Peeled ripe bananas	**135 g (4³/₄ oz), cut into 0.5-cm (¹/₄-in) thick slices**
Lemon juice	**1¹/₃ Tbsp**
Filling	
Cream cheese	**435 g (14¹/₄ oz)**
Light brown sugar	**95 g (3¹/₄ oz)**
Corn flour (cornstarch)	**2¹/₄ Tbsp, sifted**
Vanilla essence	**¹/₃ tsp**
Eggs	**2, large**
Whipping cream	**70 ml (2¹/₂ fl oz)**
Milk	**70 ml (2¹/₂ fl oz)**
Semi-sweet chocolate chips	**60 g (2 oz)**

Prepare round Classic Digestive Crust with walnuts.

Prepare caramelised bananas. In a medium saucepan, melt butter and sugar over medium heat until sugar has dissolved and mixture begins to brown. Add banana slices and stir-fry until caramelised but still firm. Lower heat and add lemon juice, then stir for another 2 minutes. Remove from heat and cool.

Preheat oven to 160°C (325°F).

Prepare filling. With an electric mixer, beat cream cheese and light brown sugar at medium speed until creamy. Beat in sifted corn flour and vanilla essence until smooth. Lower speed and add eggs, 1 at a time, mixing until just incorporated. Gradually add whipping cream and milk until well mixed. Fold in chocolate chips.

Pour half of filling onto prepared crust. Arrange banana slices in an even layer, 1-cm (¹/₂-in) away from edge of pan. Cover with remaining filling.

Bake in a water bath for 1 hour 10 minutes–1 hour 30 minutes, or until edge of filling is set and centre is slightly wobbly. Turn off oven and leave cheesecake inside for 30 minutes with oven door closed. Prop open door and leave for another 30 minutes. Remove cheesecake from oven and cool on a wire rack.

Refrigerate for at least 6 hours before unmoulding and serving.

Makes an 18-cm (7-in) round cheesecake

Almond Toffee Buttercrunch Cheesecake

The sweet and crunchy bits in this ultra-rich cheesecake come from Almond Roca, a popular American confection made of buttered toffee coated in milk chocolate and almonds.

23-cm (9-in) round Classic Digestive Crust (see pg 145)	**1**
Almond Roca candies	**20 pieces, total about 265 g (9¹/₄ oz)**
Filling	
Cream cheese	**680 g (1¹/₂ lb)**
Sweetened condensed milk	**1 can, 400 g (14 oz)**
Vanilla essence	**1 tsp**
Eggs	**3, large**
Ganache Topping	
Dark chocolate	**100 g (3¹/₂ oz)**
Whipping cream	**100 ml (3¹/₃ fl oz)**

Prepare round Classic Digestive Crust.

With a sharp knife, chop Almond Roca candies into small pieces. Reserve half for topping.

Preheat oven to 150°C (300°F).

Prepare filling. With an electric mixer, beat cream cheese at medium speed until creamy. Gradually beat in sweetened condensed milk and vanilla essence until smooth. Lower speed and add eggs, 1 at a time, mixing until just incorporated. Fold in chopped candies.

Pour filling onto prepared crust. Bake for 1 hour 50 minutes–2 hours 10 minutes, or until centre of filling is set. Turn off oven and leave cheesecake inside for 45 minutes with oven door closed. Prop open door and leave for another 45 minutes. Remove cheesecake from oven and cool on a wire rack.

Prepare ganache topping. Place chopped chocolate in a small bowl. Boil cream and pour over chopped chocolate. Let stand for 1 minute. Stir gently until smooth. When cool, spread topping evenly on top of cheesecake with a spatula. Sprinkle reserved chopped candies on top.

Refrigerate for at least 6 hours before unmoulding and serving.

Makes a 23-cm (9-in) round cheesecake

Golden Cheesecake Squares

Prepare these fabulous dessert squares with good-quality, clear liquid honey. For an extra boost in flavour, drizzle the bars with more honey before devouring them.

Sweet Crust Dough
  for a 23-cm (9-in)
  round (see pg 148)   **1 portion**

Filling

Cream cheese	**585 g (1 lb 4³/₄ oz)**
Light brown sugar	**95 g (3¹/₄ oz)**
Honey	**95 g (3¹/₄ oz)**
Vanilla essence	**¹/₂ tsp**
Corn flour (cornstarch)	**3 Tbsp, sifted**
Eggs	**3, medium**
Whipping cream	**95 ml (3¹/₆ fl oz)**
Milk	**95 ml (3¹/₆ fl oz)**

Garnish (optional)
Raisins

Prepare Sweet Crust Dough for lining the bottom of a 23-cm (9-in) square pan.

Preheat oven to 175°C (350°F).

Butter and flour the base of a 23-cm (9-in) square cake pan. On a floured surface, roll dough to approximately a 23-cm (9-in) square. Transfer dough to pan and line bottom evenly. Prick base all over with a fork. Bake shell for 15–20 minutes, or until very lightly browned. Leave to cool completely on a wire rack.

Prepare filling. With an electric mixer, beat cream cheese and light brown sugar at medium speed until creamy. Beat in honey, vanilla essence and sifted corn flour until smooth. Lower speed and add eggs, 1 at a time, mixing until just incorporated. Gradually add whipping cream and milk until well mixed.

Pour filling onto prepared crust. Bake in a water bath for 1 hour 10 minutes–1 hour 30 minutes, or until edge of filling is set and centre is slightly wobbly. Turn off oven and leave cheesecake inside for 30 minutes with oven door closed. Prop open door and leave for another 30 minutes. Remove cheesecake from oven and cool on a wire rack.

Refrigerate for at least 6 hours. Cut into squares and decorate with raisins before serving, if desired.

Makes thirty-six 4-cm (1¹/₂-in) squares

Herbs, Spices and Others

Lemon and Thyme Mascarpone Cheese Sorbet with
  Homemade Fresh Fruit Salsa *118*

Mexican Chocolate Delight *121*

Almond-crusted Darjeeling Tea Cheesecake *122*

Tiramisu au Thé Vert *125*

Candied Ginger Cheese Tart *127*

Milk Chocolate-Mascarpone Crème with
  Earl Grey Tea Granita *128*

Cream Cheese Vanilla Panna Cotta with Coffee Gelée *131*

Lemon and Thyme Mascarpone Cheese Sorbet with Homemade Fresh Fruit Salsa

The classic combination of lemon and thyme is recreated in this aromatic and refreshing sorbet. Serve the sorbet on its own or with the fruit salsa.

Lemon and Thyme Mascarpone Sorbet

Castor (superfine) sugar	**165 g (5³/₄ oz)**
Water	**165 ml (5¹/₂ fl oz)**
Fresh thyme	**about 7 sprigs**
Mascarpone cheese	**250 g (8³/₄ oz)**
Lemon juice	**1¹/₂ Tbsp**

Fruit Salsa

Kiwi	**1, medium, peeled and diced**
Mango	**1, medium, peeled and diced**
Diced strawberries	**100 g (3¹/₂ oz)**
Mint leaves	**about 8, finely chopped**
Lemon zest	**1 tsp**
Lemon juice	**1 Tbsp**
Castor (superfine) sugar	**2 tsp**
Ground ginger	**¹/₄ tsp**

Prepare sorbet. In a small saucepan over medium heat, bring sugar and water to the boil. Lower heat and simmer until slightly thickened. Remove from heat and immediately add thyme sprigs. Leave to cool, then cover and refrigerate syrup overnight. Strain and discard thyme sprigs. Keep chilled.

In a medium bowl, stir mascarpone cheese to soften. Gradually whisk in chilled thyme syrup and lemon juice until smooth. Cover and refrigerate for 1 hour.

Pour mixture into an ice cream machine and churn according to the manufacturer's directions. Transfer sorbet into an airtight container and freeze for 6 hours or until firm.

Prepare fruit salsa. Stir together chopped kiwi, mango, strawberries, mint leaves and lemon zest. Set aside.

In a non-reactive saucepan, heat lemon juice, sugar and ground ginger over medium heat until sugar dissolves. Lower heat and add fruit mixture. Toss until slightly softened and well coated in syrup, about 1 minute. Leave to cool, then cover and refrigerate for up to 24 hours before serving with sorbet.

Makes 4–6 servings

Mexican Chocolate Delight

Mexican chocolate, commonly used in hot drinks, consists of dark chocolate flavoured with cinnamon. Occasionally, they are flavoured with other spices and include nuts.

Spiced Chocolate Mousse

Whipping cream	**250 ml (8 fl oz / 1 cup)**
Ground cinnamon	**$^1/_2$ tsp**
Icing (confectioner's) sugar	**$3^1/_3$ Tbsp**
Cream cheese	**60 g (2 oz)**
Castor (superfine) sugar	**1 Tbsp**
Dark chocolate	**35 g ($1^1/_4$ oz), melted and still slightly warm**

Dark Chocolate Ganache with Cointreau

Dark chocolate	**45 g ($1^1/_2$ oz), finely chopped**
Whipping cream	**3 Tbsp**
Cointreau	**$1^1/_4$ tsp**

Garnish (optional)

Cocoa powder	

Prepare spiced chocolate mousse. Stir together whipping cream, ground cinnamon and icing sugar in a mixing bowl. Set aside in the refrigerator to chill for 30 minutes.

Meanwhile, prepare ganache. Place chopped chocolate in a small bowl. Boil cream and pour over chopped chocolate. Stir gently until smooth. Stir in Cointreau. Set aside.

For spiced chocolate mousse, beat cream cheese and sugar until creamy. Blend in melted chocolate until smooth.

Whip chilled cinnamon cream until medium peaks form. Fold half of cream into chocolate-cheese mixture until just incorporated. Store remaining whipped cream in the refrigerator for topping.

To assemble, arrange 6 small glasses on a tray and half-fill with mousse. Top with ganache, then finish with remaining mousse. Refrigerate for 1 hour.

Transfer remaining whipped cinnamon cream into a pastry bag fitted with a 1-cm ($^1/_2$-in) tip and pipe on top of mousse. Refrigerate for another 3 hours.

Dust with cocoa powder and decorate as desired to serve.

Makes about 6 servings

Almond-crusted Darjeeling Tea Cheesecake

Darjeeling tea originates from northern India. Its exotic flavour lightly perfumes this cheesecake and pairs well with the delicate nuttiness of the almond crust. Use loose tea leaves as they are of better quality than tea bags.

23-cm (9-in) round Classic Digestive Crust with sliced almonds (see pg 145)	**1**
Filling	
Milk	**180 ml (6 fl oz / ³/₄ cup)**
Darjeeling tea leaves	**75 g (2³/₄ oz)**
Cream cheese	**825 g (1³/₄ lb 1 oz)**
Castor (superfine) sugar	**155 g (5¹/₂ oz)**
Corn flour (cornstarch)	**3¹/₄ Tbsp, sifted**
Vanilla essence	**²/₃ tsp**
Eggs	**4, medium**
Whipping cream	**120 ml (4 fl oz)**

Prepare round Classic Digestive Crust with sliced almonds.

In a medium saucepan over medium heat, bring milk to a gentle boil. Remove from heat and immediately add in tea leaves. Steep for 3 minutes. Strain milk mixture, extracting as much liquid from leaves as possible. Leave to cool. Discard tea leaves.

Preheat oven to 160°C (325°F).

With an electric mixer, beat cream cheese and sugar at medium speed until creamy. Beat in sifted corn flour and vanilla essence until smooth. Lower speed and add eggs, 1 at a time, mixing until just incorporated. Gradually add whipping cream and milk mixture until well mixed.

Pour filling onto prepared crust. Bake in a water bath for 1 hour 40 minutes–2 hours, or until edges of filling are set and centre is slightly wobbly. Turn off oven and leave cheesecake inside for 45 minutes with oven door closed. Prop open door and leave for another 45 minutes. Remove cheesecake from oven and cool on a wire rack.

Refrigerate for at least 8 hours before unmoulding and serving.

Makes a 23-cm (9-in) round cheesecake

Tiramisu Au Thé Vert

Although tiramisu is traditionally made with mascarpone cheese, we've used cream cheese in this recipe as its flavour better complements the aroma of the green tea.

Green Tea Sponge Cake

Japanese green tea powder	**2 tsp**
Warm water	**1¹/₃ Tbsp**
Cake flour	**50 g (1³/₄ oz)**
Eggs	**2, yolks and whites separated**
Castor (superfine) sugar	**60 g (2 oz)**
Vanilla essence	**¹/₄ tsp**
Butter	**2¹/₃ Tbsp, melted and cooled**

Green Tea Syrup

Japanese green tea powder	**1¹/₂ tsp**
Warm water	**1 Tbsp**
Sugar syrup (see pg 152)	**6 Tbsp**

Preheat oven to 180°C (350°F).

Line the bottom of an 18-cm (7-in) round cake pan with baking paper.

Prepare sponge. Dissolve green tea powder in warm water. Sift cake flour and set aside. In a small bowl, whisk egg yolks, 2 tsp sugar and vanilla essence until pale yellow and thickened. Whisk in green tea mixture.

In a separate, clean mixing bowl, whisk egg whites with an electric mixer at medium speed until foamy. Increase speed to high and gradually add remaining sugar. Whisk until firm and glossy peaks form. Fold one-third of whites into egg yolk mixture to lighten. Gently fold in remaining whites, followed by cake flour. Fold in melted butter until just incorporated.

Pour batter into prepared cake pan and bake for 20–25 minutes, or until top is browned and springs back when lightly pressed. Leave to cool in pan for 10 minutes. Unmould and cool completely on a wire rack. Slice horizontally into 2 even layers.

Prepare green tea syrup. Dissolve green tea powder in warm water. Stir in sugar syrup. Set aside.

Prepare filling. In a small saucepan, soak gelatine in 2¹/₃ Tbsp water for 10 minutes. Warm over low heat until gelatine has dissolved. Leave to cool. Dissolve green tea powder into 1 Tbsp warm water.

continued on next page

Filling

Gelatine powder	**1 Tbsp**
Water	**2¹/₃ Tbsp**
Japanese green tea powder	**1¹/₂ tsp**
Warm water	**1 Tbsp**
Egg yolks	**4, large**
Castor (superfine) sugar	**55 g (2 oz)**
Cream cheese	**135 g (4³/₄ oz), softened**
Whipping cream	**155 ml (5 fl oz)**

Garnish (optional)

Chocolate shavings

Chocolate pieces

Place egg yolks and sugar in a heatproof mixing bowl and set over a pot of simmering water. Whisk until yolks become pale and glossy. Remove from heat. Stir in gelatine and green tea mixtures until well mixed. Gradually blend egg yolk mixture into softened cream cheese until smooth.

In a separate mixing bowl, beat whipping cream until medium-soft peaks form. Fold one-third of cream into cream cheese mixture to lighten. Gently fold in remaining cream until just incorporated.

Wrap the base of an 18-cm (7-in) round cake ring that has a removable bottom with aluminium foil and place on a baking tray. This will prevent the syrup or mousse from seeping out and creating a mess on the tray when assembling and chilling the cake.

To assemble, place a layer of sponge into prepared cake ring and moisten with green tea syrup. Pour half of filling into ring. Lightly press second layer of sponge on filling and moisten with more syrup. Pour in remaining filling. Refrigerate for at least 4 hours before unmoulding.

Decorate with chocolate shavings and chocolate pieces, if desired, before serving.

Makes an 18-cm (7-in) round cheesecake

Candied Ginger Cheese Tart

Ginger contributes a mild warmth to this rich cheesecake tart. Bake this tart the day before serving to allow the flavours to mellow. Serve in small wedges with a side of fresh fruit, if desired.

Sweet Crust Dough for a 23-cm (9-in) round (see pg 148)	**1 portion**
Filling	
Cream cheese	**400 g (14 oz)**
Castor (superfine) sugar	**75 g (2³/₄ oz)**
Vanilla essence	**²/₃ tsp**
Eggs	**2, large**
Whipping cream	**2 Tbsp**
Ground ginger	**1¹/₂ tsp**
Crystallised or candied ginger	**60 g (2 oz), finely chopped**

Prepare Sweet Crust Dough.

Butter and flour a 23-cm (9-in) round tart pan with a removable bottom. On a floured surface, roll dough to approximately 0.5-cm (¹/₂-in) thick. Transfer dough to pan, lining bottom and sides evenly. Trim off excess dough with a paring knife. Prick base all over with a fork and refrigerate for at least 1 hour before using.

Preheat oven to 175°C (350°F).

Prepare filling. With an electric mixer, beat cream cheese, sugar and vanilla essence on medium speed until creamy. Lower speed and add eggs, 1 at a time, mixing until just incorporated. Beat in whipping cream and ground ginger until well mixed.

Pour filling into chilled tart shell and sprinkle chopped crystallised or candied ginger evenly on top. Bake for 35–40 minutes, or until filling is set and golden. Remove from oven and leave to cool in pan on a wire rack.

Remove tart pan and transfer tart to a serving plate. Refrigerate overnight before serving.

Makes a 23-cm (9-in) round tart

Milk Chocolate-Mascarpone Crème with Earl Grey Tea Granita

The wonderful contrast of the slushy granita and the smooth mascarpone crème can be clearly seen through the dessert glasses. Prepare the components the day before and it will only take a matter of minutes to assemble before serving.

Earl Grey Tea Granita

Freshly brewed strong Earl Grey tea	**300 ml (10 fl oz / 1^1/$_4$ cups), very hot**
Castor (superfine) sugar	**60 g (2 oz)**

Milk Chocolate-Mascarpone Crème

Milk chocolate	**215 g (7^1/$_2$ oz), melted and still slightly warm**
Vanilla essence	**^{3}/$_4$ tsp**
Mascarpone cheese	**200 g (7 oz), softened**
Whipping cream	**300 ml (10 fl oz / 1^1/$_4$ cups), chilled**

Garnish (optional)

Milk chocolate shavings	

Prepare granita the day before. Ensure tea is very hot. Stir sugar in to dissolve completely. Leave to cool then pour into a freezer-safe container. Cover and freeze.

After 2 hours, remove container from freezer and coarsely chop mixture with a metal scraper or knife. Toss mixture thoroughly. Cover and return to freezer. Repeat process thrice, once every 2 hours. Store in freezer.

Prepare mascarpone crème. Gradually whisk melted milk chocolate and vanilla essence into mascarpone cheese until smooth.

In a separate mixing bowl, beat whipping cream until medium peaks form. Fold one-third of cream into milk chocolate mixture to lighten. Gently fold in remaining cream until just incorporated. Cover and refrigerate for 2 hours.

To assemble, arrange 6 small glasses or bowls on a tray. Remove granita from freezer and chop evenly. Briefly whisk chilled mascarpone crème to smoothen. Spoon crème into glasses, followed by granita. Garnish with milk chocolate shavings, if desired. Serve immediately.

Makes about 6 servings

Cream Cheese Vanilla Panna Cotta with Coffee Gelée

This glamorous dessert is sure to impress your guests. It requires some patience to prepare, but the end result is definitely worth it!

Cream Cheese Panna Cotta

Gelatine powder	**1^1/$_4$ Tbsp**
Water	**3 Tbsp**
Cream cheese	**200 g (7 oz), softened**
Castor (superfine) sugar	**50 g (1^3/$_4$ oz)**
Milk	**160 ml (5^1/$_3$ fl oz)**
Whipping cream	**80 ml (2^1/$_2$ fl oz)**
Vanilla essence	**^{2}/$_3$ tsp**

Coffee Gelée

Gelatine powder	**1^1/$_2$ Tbsp**
Water	**200 ml (6^2/$_3$ fl oz)**
Instant coffee granules	**2^1/$_2$ tsp**
Warm water	**75 ml (2^1/$_3$ fl oz)**
Light brown sugar	**75 g (2^1/$_2$ oz)**

Prepare cream cheese panna cotta. Soak gelatine in water for 10 minutes. Stir softened cream cheese and sugar together until smooth. Set aside.

In a medium saucepan over medium heat, heat milk and whipping cream until just about to boil. Lower heat and add cream cheese mixture, stirring constantly until smooth. Remove from heat. Stir in gelatine mixture and vanilla essence. Strain mixture and cool.

Prepare coffee gelée. Soak gelatine in 50 ml (1^2/$_3$ fl oz) water for 10 minutes. Dissolve coffee granules in warm water. Set aside.

In a medium saucepan, boil brown sugar and remaining 150 ml (5 fl oz) water over medium heat until brown sugar has completely dissolved. Remove from heat. Stir in coffee and gelatine mixtures. Leave to cool.

To assemble, arrange 6–8 small glasses on a tray and spoon 1^1/$_2$ Tbsp cream cheese mixture into each glass. Refrigerate for 30 minutes. Remove from refrigerator and spoon 1 Tbsp coffee mixture over cream cheese layer. Refrigerate for another 30 minutes. Repeat process twice, ending with coffee mixture as the top layer. Refrigerate for 3 hours before serving. Decorate as desired.

Makes 6–8 servings

On the lighter side

Ricotta Frozen Yoghurt

With only five ingredients, this low fat treat couldn't be any easier to prepare. Ricotta cheese and yoghurt give it a milky and smooth consistency, unlike other low-fat frozen products which tend to have a grainy texture.

Ricotta cheese	**190 g (6³/₄ oz), well-drained**
Plain low-fat yoghurt	**360 g (12³/₄ oz)**
Honey or maple syrup (optional)	**1¹/₂ Tbsp**
Sugar Syrup	
Castor (superfine) sugar	**120 g (4¹/₂ oz)**
Water	**150 ml (5 fl oz)**
Garnish (optional)	
Finely chopped unsalted pistachio nuts	

Prepare sugar syrup. In a small saucepan over medium heat, boil sugar and water until sugar has dissolved and mixture thickens slightly. Cool and refrigerate until thoroughly chilled.

In a blender (processor), pulse ricotta cheese, yoghurt and honey or maple syrup, if using, until smooth.

With blender running, gradually add chilled sugar syrup and process until well combined.

Pour mixture into an ice cream machine and churn according to manufacturer's directions. Transfer frozen yoghurt to an airtight container and freeze for 6 hours or until firm. Garnish as desired before serving.

Makes 6–8 servings

Silky Tofu Cheesecake

Silken tofu contributes to the custard-like texture of this cheesecake. It's hard to believe that this creamy concoction is low in fat and, thus, less threatening for your waistline!

23-cm (9-in) round Vanilla Sponge Cake (see pg 149)	**1, sliced horizontally into 2 layers**
Filling	
Gelatine powder	**2²/₃ Tbsp**
Water	**6 Tbsp**
Milk	**220 ml (7 fl oz)**
Castor (superfine) sugar	**145 g (5 oz)**
Reduced-fat cream cheese spread	**380 g (13¹/₂ oz)**
Silken tofu	**160 g (5³/₄ oz)**
Garnish (optional)	
Chocolate sauce (see pg 151)	

Prepare round Vanilla Sponge Cake. From 1 of the sponge layers, cut out 6 rounds using a 6-cm (2¹/₂-in) round cookie cutter. Reserve other layer for another use.

Prepare filling. Soak gelatine in water for 10 minutes. In a medium saucepan, warm milk and sugar over low heat until sugar has completely dissolved. Remove from heat and stir in gelatine mixture. Set aside.

In a blender (processor), purée cream cheese and silken tofu until smooth. Gradually add milk mixture and pulse until well blended. Strain filling and discard any residue. This will ensure a smooth mousse.

To assemble, place six 7.5-cm (3-in) round cake rings on a baking tray. Fill each ring until approximately 1-cm (¹/₂-in) from the top edge. Place a round of sponge on top of filling and lightly press until cake is level with the top edge. Repeat with remaining rings.

Cover top of each ring with plastic wrap to secure sponge in place. Refrigerate for at least 4 hours. Remove plastic wrap and invert ring onto a serving plate to unmould.

Decorate as desired and serve with chocolate sauce, if using.

Makes six 7.5-cm (3-in) round mini cheesecakes

Jasmine-Yoghurt Passions

This cloud-light dessert is perfect for serving after a rich meal. For variation, substitute the jasmine essence with an equal amount of orange essence.

Gelatine powder	$^1/_2$ Tbsp
Water	$1^1/_3$ Tbsp
Passion fruit purée	40 g ($1^1/_2$ oz)
Reduced-fat cream cheese spread	125 g ($4^1/_2$ oz)
Low-fat plain yoghurt	150 g ($5^1/_4$ oz)
Castor (superfine) sugar	$4^1/_2$ Tbsp
Jasmine essence	$^1/_4$ tsp
Egg whites	2, large

Garnish (optional)
Passion fruit coulis
Fresh mint leaves

In a small saucepan, soak gelatine in water for 10 minutes. Warm over low heat until gelatine has dissolved. Remove from heat and stir in passion fruit purée. Set aside.

In a medium bowl, stir cream cheese spread with a rubber spatula until smooth. Blend in yoghurt, $2^1/_2$ Tbsp sugar, jasmine essence and passion fruit mixture until well incorporated.

In a separate, clean mixing bowl, whisk egg whites with an electric mixer at medium speed until foamy. Increase speed to high and gradually add remaining sugar. Whisk until firm and glossy peaks form. Fold one-third of egg whites into cheese mixture to lighten. Gently fold in remaining egg whites until just incorporated.

To assemble, arrange 6 small glasses on a tray and divide mixture evenly among glasses. Refrigerate for 4 hours before serving. Garnish with passion fruit coulis and mint leaves, if desired.

Makes about 6 servings

Mandarin-Almond Cheesecake

This soft-set baked cheesecake is lightened with ricotta cheese and has a slightly nutty texture. It is also gluten-free, which makes it a healthier alternative to traditional baked cheesecakes.

Almond Crust

Ground almonds	**70 g (2^1/$_2$ oz)**
Light brown sugar	**1^1/$_2$ Tbsp**
Butter	**2^1/$_2$ Tbsp (1^1/$_4$ oz), melted and still warm**
Egg white	**16 g (^{1}/$_2$ oz)**

Filling

Cream cheese	**320 g (11^1/$_4$ oz)**
Ricotta cheese	**250 g (8^3/$_4$ oz), well drained**
Castor (superfine) sugar	**120 g (4^1/$_4$ oz)**
Vanilla essence	**^{2}/$_3$ tsp**
Orange juice	**2 Tbsp**
Orange zest	**1 Tbsp**
Eggs	**3, large**
Ground almonds	**45 g (1^1/$_2$ oz)**

Marmalade Glaze

Orange marmalade	**100 g (3^1/$_2$ oz)**
Water	**2 tsp**

Topping

Canned mandarin orange segments	**1 can, 310 g (11 oz), well drained**

Prepare almond crust. Mix together ground almonds, light brown sugar, melted butter and egg white. Press evenly onto the bottom of an 18-cm (7-in) round springform pan. Refrigerate for 1 hour.

Preheat oven to 180°C (350°F).

Prepare filling. With an electric mixer, beat cream cheese and ricotta at medium speed until creamy. Beat in sugar, vanilla essence, orange juice and orange zest until smooth. Lower speed and add eggs, 1 at a time, mixing until just incorporated. Fold in ground almonds.

Pour filling onto prepared crust. Bake in a water bath for 1 hour 50 minutes–2 hours 10 minutes, or until edges of filling are set and centre is slightly wobbly. Turn off oven and leave cheesecake inside for 30 minutes with oven door closed. Prop open door and leave for another 30 minutes. Remove cheesecake from oven and cool on a wire rack. Refrigerate for 6 hours or overnight before unmoulding.

Prepare glaze. In a small saucepan, warm marmalade and water over low heat until melted and smooth. Leave to cool for 10 minutes.

Arrange mandarin orange segments on top of cake and spoon glaze over. Refrigerate for 1 hour to set glaze before serving.

Makes an 18-cm (7-in) round cheesecake

Photo on following page

Mango and Lychee Ricotta Meringue Parfaits

Ricotta and egg whites lighten this dessert. As a variation to this recipe, replace the lychees and mangoes with any fruit of your choice.

Mangoes	**3, medium, ripe but still firm**
Ricotta cheese	**250 g (8³/₄ oz), well drained**
Mascarpone cheese	**200 g (7 oz)**
Castor (superfine) sugar	**55 g**
Orange zest	**1 Tbsp**
Vanilla essence	**¹/₂ tsp**
Egg whites	**2, large**
Canned lychees in syrup	**300 g (11 oz), about 16 large wholes, drained and coarsely chopped**

Garnish (optional)
Whole raspberries

Peel and cut mangoes into 1-cm (¹/₂-in) cubes.

Process ricotta, mascarpone cheese and 20 g (³/₄ oz) sugar in a blender (processor) until smooth. Transfer mixture to a large bowl. Stir in orange zest and vanilla essence.

In a separate, clean mixing bowl, whisk egg whites with an electric mixer at medium speed until foamy. Increase speed to high and gradually add remaining sugar. Whisk until firm and glossy peaks form.

Fold one-third of egg whites into ricotta mixture to lighten. Gently fold in remaining egg whites until just incorporated.

To assemble, arrange 6–8 small glasses on a tray and divide one-third of ricotta mixture among glasses. Top with mango cubes then cover with another third of ricotta mixture. Spoon in lychees, then cover with remaining ricotta mixture. Refrigerate for 4 hours before serving. Garnish with raspberries as desired.

Makes 6–8 servings

Basic Recipes

Classic Digestive Crust

A delicious crust contributes to the overall experience of eating a cheesecake. Crushed digestive biscuits bind well when mixed with melted butter, and the result is a slightly crispy and scrumptious base perfect for cheesecakes.

	18-cm (7-in) round	23-cm (9-in) round
Digestive biscuits	95 g (3^1/$_4$ oz)	160 g (5^3/$_4$ oz)
Light brown sugar	1 Tbsp	1^1/$_2$ Tbsp
Butter	50 g (1^3/$_4$ oz)	80 g (2^3/$_4$ oz)

Wrap a springform pan with a layer of aluminium foil. Place on a baking tray and set aside.

Break digestive biscuits into large chunks. Place in a blender and pulse until finely ground. Transfer to another bowl and stir in brown sugar until well mixed.

In a microwave oven, warm butter at medium power until completely melted and smooth. Pour warm butter over digestive mixture. Toss well to coat mixture with butter.

Transfer mixture to prepared pan. With your hands (you may wish to wear disposable gloves), press firmly into an even layer on the bottom of pan. Refrigerate for at least 1 hour before using.

Digestive Crust with Nuts

Jazz up the crust by adding lightly toasted chopped walnuts, pistachios, pecans, macadamias or sliced almonds. For an 18-cm (7-in) round crust, mix 2 Tbsp of your preferred nuts (or 3^1/$_2$ Tbsp for a 23-cm / 9-in round crust) together with ground digestives and brown sugar. Proceed as directed above.

Oreo Crust

This crust is extremely easy to prepare. The vanilla crème in the Oreo cookies helps bind the crumbs together.

	18-cm (7-in) round	23-cm (9-in) round
Oreo sandwich cookies	**100 g (3^1/$_2$ oz)**	**170 g (6 oz)**

Wrap a springform pan with a layer of aluminium foil. Place on a baking tray and set aside.

Break cookies into large chunks. Place in a blender and pulse until finely ground.

Transfer ground cookies to prepared pan. With your hands (you may wish to wear disposable gloves), press firmly into an even layer on the bottom of pan. Refrigerate for at least 1 hour before using.

Chocolate Crème Oreo Crust

Instead of the traditional vanilla crème Oreo cookies, use chocolate crème Oreo cookies for an even more chocolaty crust.

Sweet Crust Dough

Butter	110 g (4 oz), softened but still cool
Castor (superfine) sugar	50 g (1³/₄ oz)
Salt	¹/₄ tsp
Egg yolk	1, large
Plain (all-purpose) flour	190 g (6³/₄ oz)
Whipping cream	1 Tbsp

With an electric mixer, cream butter and sugar until well blended. Add salt and egg yolk, beating until well incorporated.

Reduce speed to low. Add flour and mix until dough is about to come together. Add cream and mix until dough is smooth. Gather dough into a ball and cover with plastic wrap. Refrigerate dough for at least 2 hours or up to 3 days.

Remove dough from refrigerator. Let soften slightly at room temperature for 10–15 minutes. Proceed as directed in specific recipe.

Makes enough dough for a 23-cm (9-in) round tart shell or six 7.5-cm (3-in) round tartlet shells.

Chocolate Sweet Crust Dough

Chilling the dough sufficiently allows the gluten to relax and prevents the dough from shrinking too much during baking.

Plain (all-purpose) flour	100 g (3¹/₂ oz)
Cocoa powder	1 Tbsp
Salt	¹/₄ tsp
Butter	55 g (2 oz), softened but still cool
Icing (confectioner's) sugar	60 g (2 oz)
Egg	¹/₂, large

Sift together flour, cocoa powder and salt. Set aside.

With an electric mixer, cream butter at low speed until smooth. Add icing sugar and mix until well incorporated.

Add egg and mix until smooth. Add flour mixture and continue mixing at low speed until dough just comes together. Gather dough into a ball and cover with plastic wrap. Refrigerate for at least 4 hours or up to 3 days.

Remove dough from refrigerator. Let soften slightly at room temperature for 10–15 minutes. Proceed as directed in specific recipe.

Makes enough dough for a 23-cm (9-in) round tart shell or six 7.5-cm (3-in) round tartlet shells

Vanilla Sponge Cake

Separating the egg whites and egg yolks gives this sponge cake its characteristic light and fluffy texture. The melted butter adds tenderness to the cake's crumb. This versatile sponge can be used as a base for a near endless variety of cakes.

	18-cm (7-in) round	23-cm (9-in) round
Cake flour	50 g (1³/₄ oz)	80 g (2³/₄ oz)
Butter	35 g (1¹/₄ oz)	55g (2 oz)
Eggs	2, medium, yolks and whites separated	3, medium, yolks and whites separated
Castor (superfine) sugar (A)	2 tsp	1¹/₄ Tbsp
Vanilla essence	¹/₄ tsp	¹/₂ tsp
Castor (superfine) sugar (B)	50 g (1³/₄ oz)	85 g (3 oz)

Method

Preheat oven to 180°C (350°F). Line bottom of the cake pan with baking paper. Sift cake flour and set aside. Melt butter and leave to cool.

In a small bowl, whisk egg yolks, sugar (A) and vanilla essence until pale yellow and thickened.

In a separate, clean mixing bowl, whisk egg whites with an electric mixer at medium speed until foamy. Increase speed to high and gradually add sugar (B). Whisk until firm and glossy peaks form. Fold one-third of whites into egg yolk mixture. Gently fold in remaining whites, followed by cake flour. Fold in melted butter until just incorporated.

Pour batter into pan and level with a spatula. Bake 18-cm (7-in) sponge for 20–25 minutes and 23-cm (9-in) sponge for 25–30 minutes. Remove from oven and leave to cool in pan for 10 minutes. Run a metal spatula around inside of pan to loosen cake. Unmould and cool completely on a wire rack. Remove baking paper and use as directed in specific recipe.

Refrigerate any extra sponge, well covered with plastic wrap, for up to 3 days, or freeze for up to 4 weeks.

Chocolate Sponge Cake

This chocolate version of the vanilla sponge cake is just as delicious and pairs well with any chocolate-based cake or dessert.

	18-cm (7-in) round	23-cm (9-in) round
Cake flour	35 g (1¹/₄ oz)	60 g (2 oz)
Cocoa powder	1¹/₄ Tbsp	2¹/₄ Tbsp
Butter	35 g (1¹/₄ oz)	55 g (2 oz)
Eggs	2, medium, yolks and whites separated	3, medium, yolks and whites separated
Castor (superfine) sugar (A)	2 tsp	1¹/₄ Tbsp
Vanilla essence	¹/₄ tsp	¹/₂ tsp
Castor (superfine) sugar (B)	60 g (2 oz)	100 g (3¹/₂ oz)

Preheat oven to 180°C (350°F). Line bottom of pan with baking paper. Sift together cake flour and cocoa powder. Set aside. Melt butter and leave to cool.

In a small bowl, whisk egg yolks, sugar (A) and vanilla essence until pale yellow and thickened.

In a separate, clean mixing bowl, whisk egg whites with an electric mixer at medium speed until foamy. Increase speed to high and gradually add sugar (B). Whisk until firm and glossy peaks form. Fold one-third of whites into egg yolk mixture to lighten. Gently fold in remaining whites, followed by flour mixture. Fold in melted butter until just incorporated.

Pour batter into pan and level with a spatula. Bake 18-cm (7-in) sponge for 20–25 minutes and 23-cm (9-in) sponge for 25–30 minutes. Leave to cool in pan for 10 minutes. Run a metal spatula around inside of pan to loosen cake. Unmould and cool completely on a wire rack. Remove baking paper and use as directed in specific recipe.

Chocolate Sheet Sponge Cake

To make a chocolate sheet sponge cake, line a 23-cm (9-in) square baking tray with baking paper. Prepare batter for an 18-cm (7-in) round Chocolate Sponge Cake as directed on pg 150. Spread batter evenly on tray with a spatula and bake at 180°C (350°F) for 12–15 minutes. Run a metal spatula along the inside of tray to loosen cake. Unmould and cool completely on a wire rack. Remove baking paper and use as directed in specific recipe.

Chocolate Sauce

This silky-smooth chocolate sauce, enriched with butter, is perfect when drizzled over anything sweet. Use this versatile sauce when still warm or at room temperature.

Milk	**4 Tbsp**
Whipping cream	**4 Tbsp**
Butter	**2 tsp**
Dark chocolate	**130 g (5³/₄ oz), finely chopped**

In a medium saucepan, heat milk, whipping cream and butter over medium heat until it comes to a gentle boil. Remove from heat and immediately add chopped chocolate. Let stand for 1 minute. Gently stir until chocolate has melted and mixture is smooth. Leave to cool to desired temperature before using.

Store sauce in the refrigerator, covered, for up to 1 week.

Makes about 250 ml (8 fl oz) sauce

Chocolate Liqueur Sauce

Give this sauce extra punch by stirring in 2 tsp of your favourite liqueur when the sauce is still warm. Rum, Cointreau and kirsch are some of our favourites that pair extremely well with this sauce.

Sugar Syrup

This simple sugar syrup works wonders. When brushed on sponge cakes, it makes them extra delicious and keeps them moist for days. Make a large quantity, stash it in the refrigerator and it'll keep for a month or two.

Castor (superfine) or granulated sugar	**100 g (3¹/₂ oz)**
Water	**250 ml (8 fl oz / 1 cup)**

In a medium saucepan, boil sugar and water, stirring occasionally, until sugar has completely dissolved. Leave to cool completely at room temperature.

Store cooled syrup in an airtight glass jar in the refrigerator. The amount of syrup to use for brushing sponge layers is entirely up to you to decide. Use more syrup if you like your cakes drenched and moist, or less if you prefer them to be mildly sweet. You can double or triple the recipe if you wish to make a larger quantity.

Makes 250–300 ml (8–10 fl oz) syrup

Sweetened Whipped Cream

Garnish any dessert with this delectable sweetened whipped cream, or use it as an accompaniment with ice creams. To make it easier to whip, chill the cream and the utensils before using.

Whipping cream	**250 ml (8 fl oz / 1 cup)**
Icing (confectioner's) sugar	**30 g (1 oz), sifted**
Vanilla essence (optional)	**¹/₄ tsp**

Place whipping cream in a large mixing bowl and refrigerate, together with beater or wire whisk, for about 1 hour or until thoroughly chilled.

Whip cream with chilled beater or wire whisk at medium speed. Gradually add sifted icing sugar, followed by vanilla essence, if desired. When cream starts to thicken, lower speed to prevent over beating. Continue beating until cream holds medium-soft peaks. It should be thick, light and fluffy. Use immediately.

Makes about 500 ml (16 fl oz / 2 cups) whipped cream

Tips and Techniques

Mise en Place (Put into Place)

Being organised is the key to yielding better results. Having all your ingredients and equipment ready before embarking on any baking process allows you to concentrate on the task ahead. The process will be smoother and more enjoyable, and you will be less likely to make mistakes.

Measuring Ingredients

Baking and cooking are different. In baking, key ingredients such as flour, gelatine and leavening agents must be accurately measured or your cakes may go awry! We recommend using a digital scale for weighing dry ingredients and a measuring jug for liquid ingredients. Place the jug on a flat surface to read the measure. All ingredients should be at room temperature unless otherwise stated in the recipe.

Preparing the Filling

You may prepare the recipes either using an electric mixer or by hand. For baked cheesecakes, take care not to over-beat the filling, especially when adding eggs and other liquid ingredients. Over-beating incorporates excessive air, which causes the filling to rise during baking and collapse upon cooling. Scraping the sides and bottom of your mixing bowl and beaters in between the addition of ingredients helps prevent ingredients from lumping and ensures a smooth filling. Stop the mixer once the ingredients have just been incorporated.

Oven and Baking Times

All recipes in this collection were tested with a conventional home oven. Position the rack in the middle of the oven and preheat for 10–15 minutes before baking. Rotate your cakes or cookies at the halfway time to ensure even baking.

Timing is essential. Check for doneness at the lower end of the time range. Care has been taken to provide baking times as accurately as possible, but they may need to be adjusted according to individual ovens. All ovens, even the same brand and models, heat up differently. It is important to pay attention and use your sense of judgment to determine the doneness of a baked product.

Baking Using a Water Bath

Place the springform pan, with the filling already poured in and wrapped with aluminium foil on the outside (in case leakage of the filling occurs), in a deep roasting tray. Pour hot water into the tray up to the halfway mark of the pan before placing in the oven. (Alternatively, place the pan on the oven rack and set a tray of hot water at the bottom of the oven.) The steam from the water bath bakes the cheesecake slowly and evenly to obtain a smooth and creamy texture. If the water level runs low halfway through baking, refill with hot water to avoid lowering the temperature too drastically.

Unmoulding and Slicing Cheesecakes

To transfer the baked cheesecake to a cake board or serving platter, grease and line the bottom of a cake pan that has a removable bottom with baking paper before pressing in the crust. When ready to unmould (the cheesecake should be thoroughly chilled), run a thin-bladed knife around the inside of the ring to loosen the sides. Remove the ring and invert the cheesecake, with the bottom attachment still at its base, onto a wire rack. Briefly use a hairdryer to blow hot air over the bottom attachment to loosen it, then carefully remove the attachment. Place a cake board or plate on top and turn the cheesecake over.

To unmould a mousse cheesecake, remove the aluminium foil and place the cake ring on a cake board or serving platter. Use a hairdryer to blow hot air around the outside edge to warm the ring. Carefully lift the ring upwards to remove.

To obtain neatly sliced cheesecakes similar to those in restaurants and cafes, use a hot, dry knife when cutting. Wipe the knife clean and re-warm it in between cuts.

Storage

For freshness, prepare these desserts on or the day before serving. Cheesecakes are best made on the day before serving to allow the flavours to ripen. Store baked cheesecakes, covered, in the refrigerator for up to 5 days, or in the freezer for up to 4 weeks (without any toppings or garnishes). Mousse cheesecakes, layered desserts and tarts are best consumed within 3 days. Frozen desserts can be kept in the freezer for up to 1 week. Cover cakes and desserts well to prevent absorption of odours.

Tricks of the Trade

Slip-ups do happen, despite all the preventive measures you have taken. Even experienced bakers make mistakes, so don't fret! If your cheesecake cracks during cooling, disguise it by topping the cake with frosting, sweetened whipped cream, fruit, glaze or chocolate ganache. If the cake becomes blotched while unmoulding, cover the blotched sides with cookie or biscuit crumbs, toasted chopped or sliced nuts. Do not be discouraged as you will get better with experience. Practice makes perfect!

Essential Ingredients

Cheese

Cream cheese is most commonly used in cheesecakes and desserts because of its distinctively smooth and creamy texture. It is made from cow's milk and has a 33 per cent fat content. Other common cheeses used are mascarpone and ricotta cheese.

Mascarpone is a soft and sweet triple cream cheese, with 50–60 per cent butterfat. Popularised by the famous Italian dessert tiramisu, it has the texture of clotted cream and its rich and buttery taste makes it ideal for use in fillings or for serving with fresh fruit.

Ricotta is a whey cheese that is firm and has a slightly grainy texture. Drain ricotta overnight by placing in a fine-meshed sieve, covered, in the refrigerator before using.

Chocolate and Cocoa

Check the labels! Purchase good quality chocolate that contains cocoa butter, not vegetable fat. Dark chocolate contains 55–60 per cent cocoa. Milk chocolate is milder and creamier and contains 35–40 per cent cocoa. White chocolate has no cocoa content and is made with cocoa butter, sweeteners and flavourings.

To melt chocolate, break it into smaller pieces, place in a microwave-safe container and heat in a microwave oven at medium power for about 1 minute. Thereafter, heat at 15 second intervals, checking and stirring between intervals until completely melted and smooth. Take care not to overheat chocolate as this will render it unusable.

Use natural, unsweetened cocoa in recipes that call for cocoa powder.

Corn Flour (Cornstarch)

In pastry-making, corn flour is used as a thickening agent. It gives baked cheesecakes structure and prevents them from cracking and collapsing. Because of its neutral taste, it will not affect the flavour of the cheesecake.

Dairy, Eggs and Butter

Use full-fat milk, not low-fat or skimmed milk, in these recipes. Use dairy whipping cream that contains 35 per cent butterfat. If the cream needs to be whipped, chill it thoroughly so that it will thicken easily. Do not over whip the cream as it will turn grainy which makes it difficult to fold into mixtures.

Use the freshest eggs possible and store them in the refrigerator to preserve their freshness. Large eggs should weigh 56–60 g (2 oz) and medium eggs 50–55 g (1^1/$_2$ oz). The weight excludes the egg shell.

Butter is preferred in baked goods and desserts because of its exceptional flavour. Melt butter in the microwave oven at medium power. You may substitute butter with margarine, but the flavour will be compromised.

Fruit and Fruit Purées

Ready-prepared frozen fruit purées are increasingly used in pastry-making because they help to save time. A wide variety of flavours are available at baking supply stores. Thaw the amount required in the refrigerator overnight and bring to room temperature before using. Use fresh fruit, freshly squeezed juices and freshly grated zest, wherever appropriate.

Gelatine

Use unflavoured gelatine powder and soak it in cold water for at least 10 minutes before using. Gelatine can also be melted in a double-boiler or over very low heat. Do not overheat gelatine as this weakens its gelling properties.

Liqueur

We like to use a hint of liqueur, wherever possible, to add warmth and flavour to sauces and desserts. You may omit it entirely or substitute with an equal amount of liquid, such as fruit juice, water or milk.

Nuts

Nuts impart a prominent flavour and texture to cakes and desserts. Store them in the refrigerator or freezer as nut oils go rancid easily. To toast nuts, spread them evenly on a baking tray and bake in an oven preheated to 180°C (350°F) for 5–10 minutes, or until lightly browned.

Sugar

Castor (superfine) sugar dissolves more easily into batters because it has a finer grain compared to granulated table sugar. In most of these recipes, you can successfully replace castor sugar with light brown sugar, but do take note that light brown sugar contains molasses which will impart a smoky, caramel-like flavour to your desserts.

Cream Cheese

Ricotta Cheese

Mascarpone Cheese

Essential Equipment

Always purchase good-quality baking ware and equipment—it is extremely worthwhile! Don't shortchange yourself and your cakes by purchasing cheap, inferior equipment. They damage easily and do not distribute heat properly, thus affecting the outcome of your baked goods.

Baking Ware

A wide variety of pans and baking ware is available. Purchase good-quality silver-coloured baking ware as they distribute heat more evenly than dark-coloured ones. Springform pans and cake rings are most commonly used for cheesecakes. Other cakes and desserts will require loaf pans, tart and tartlet pans (preferably with removable bottoms), muffin tins, glasses and ramekins. Baking trays or sheets are required for cookies and can also be used as a base for cake rings. A large, deep roasting tray is ideal for preparing water baths.

Blender (Processor)

A blender is fast, efficient and almost indispensable in any modern kitchen. Use it to chop nuts, purée fruit and grind cookies or biscuits for your cheesecake crusts.

Cooling Racks

Placing freshly baked cakes and biscuits on wire cooling racks ensure that there is sufficient air circulation around the goods to help them cool faster and more evenly. This, in turn, prevents sogginess in cakes and biscuits.

Cookie Cutters

You will require metal cookie cutters for cutting rounds of tart dough, as well as mini sponge cake rounds for petite desserts. You can also use the rim of glasses or bowls of the diameter specified in the recipe.

Hairdryer

A hairdryer makes unmolding mousse cheesecakes a breeze. It is also useful for releasing the bottom attachment of a springform pan from baked cheesecakes.

Ice Cream Machine

An electric ice cream machine is essential for making good-quality ice creams as the churning action gives it an airy, smooth texture. For home-made ice creams, a machine with a 1 litre (32 fl oz / 4 cups) capacity is sufficient.

Knives

Sharp, thin-bladed knives are handy for paring, slicing and dicing fruit, trimming excess tart dough and unmolding and slicing cheesecakes. To slice sponge cakes into horizontal layers, use a long, serrated knife.

Palette knives have blunt and flexible steel blades. They are useful for sliding underneath cheesecakes to transfer them from cake board to serving platter.

Measuring Scales and Rulers

Electronic weighing scales are much more accurate in weighing dry ingredients compared to analog scales. They are easily available in your local baking supply store and are relatively inexpensive. Use a measuring jug, with at least a 500 ml (16 fl oz / 2 cups) capacity for measuring liquid ingredients. For small amounts of ingredients, use teaspoon and tablespoon measures. Do keep a ruler solely for baking purposes in the kitchen for measuring and trimming straight lines and edges.

Mixers

A good and reliable electric mixer is fundamental, especially if you are an avid home baker. Although we recommend a standing heavy-duty mixer, a good hand-held electric mixer works perfectly well too. If you prefer, you can prepare the recipes by hand, which will involve some elbow grease.

Mixing Bowls

It is essential to have a set of stainless steel or glass bowls in a variety of sizes in your kitchen. Do not use aluminium bowls as they are reactive and may cause discolouration in cake batters. Glass bowls double up as microwavable containers for melting chocolate and butter, as well as thawing cold cream cheese.

Non-reactive Cookware

Non-reactive cookware may be made of stainless steel, glass or enamel. They are poor conductors of heat and will not react chemically with food.

Reactive cookware is made of materials such as aluminium and copper that react chemically with food. Such cookware may affect the taste and colour of the ingredients it comes into contact with.

Ovens

All the recipes in this book have been tested in a conventional electric oven. Calibrate your oven regularly with an oven thermometer to ensure accuracy, and always preheat your oven for at least 10–15 minutes before baking.

Use a microwave oven for melting ingredients such as chocolate and butter, or for thawing cold cream cheese by warming it at low power for 2–3 minutes.

Baking Paper and Aluminium Foil

Aluminium foil is used to wrap the outside of springform pans to prevent leakage of the cheesecake filling during baking.

Baking paper is useful for lining cake pans and baking trays to ensure easy removal of cakes and cookies after baking.

Pastry Brush

Use a soft-bristled brush when moistening sponge cake layers and glazing cakes and tarts to prevent unsightly marks on your cakes and desserts.

Piping Bags and Tips

Piping bags are versatile tools—use them to pipe batters, whipped cream and mousses. We use disposable piping bags as they save us the hassle of cleaning up. Plain round piping tips are required in some of the recipes, but if you like, use decorative tips for piping garnishes on your desserts.

Rolling Pins

All hands come in different sizes, so choose a rolling pin of a suitable length, weight and diameter that is comfortable for your grip. We find that tubular rolling pins without handles are easier to control.

Service and Tableware

Cake boards made with sturdy cardboard are ideal bases for holding cakes. If you are a seasoned baker and enjoy entertaining, keep an inventory of beautiful, decorative glasses, plates and large platters—they are the 'canvas' for showcasing and flaunting your mouthwatering treats!

Spatulas and Wire Whisks

These are must-have tools for any baker. Use sturdy, heatproof (flameproof) rubber or silicone spatulas, and have at least two different sizes on hand. They are ideal for folding, mixing, levelling and scraping batters. Small metal spatulas are handy for decorative work such as frosting and spreading ganaches.

Wire whisks are essential for whipping ingredients like cream and egg whites by hand. Have a few sizes of whisks on hand as well.

Storage Containers

Store your cakes and desserts in sturdy cardboard cake boxes or airtight containers to prevent them from drying out. Disposable containers are handy in the case of leftovers (which we doubt!) so that your guests can have the pleasure of bringing your delicious creations home.

Strainers and Sieves

Use a fine-meshed drum sieve for sifting flours and icing (confectioner's) sugar, and a medium-meshed sieve for draining fruits and ricotta cheese, as well as straining mixtures. A small, fine-meshed sieve is ideal for dusting icing sugar or cocoa powder on cakes and desserts.

Timers

A reliable timer is essential—an extra couple of minutes in the oven could mean tough and dry cakes!

Wooden Skewers

Test the doneness of cakes with a wooden skewer. It is longer than a toothpick which makes it safer to use and can be inserted deeper into the cake batter.

Zesters and Peelers

Use peelers which have rust-proof metal blades. Besides grating citrus zests, zesters are equally useful in grating chocolate finely over cakes for decoration.

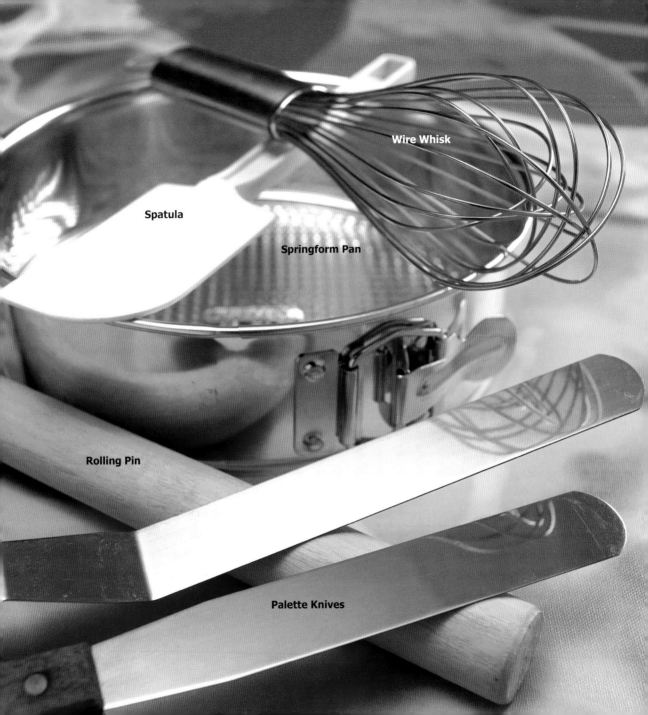

Wire Whisk

Spatula

Springform Pan

Rolling Pin

Palette Knives

Weights and Measures

Quantities for this book are given in Metric and American (spoon and cup) measures. Standard spoon and cup measurements used are: 1 tsp = 5 ml, 1 Tbsp = 15 ml, 1 cup = 250 ml. All measures are level unless otherwise stated.

LIQUID AND VOLUME MEASURES

Metric	Imperial	American
5 ml	$^1/_6$ fl oz	1 teaspoon
10 ml	$^1/_3$ fl oz	1 dessertspoon
15 ml	$^1/_2$ fl oz	1 tablespoon
60 ml	2 fl oz	$^1/_4$ cup (4 tablespoons)
85 ml	$2^1/_2$ fl oz	$^1/_3$ cup
90 ml	3 fl oz	$^3/_8$ cup (6 tablespoons)
125 ml	4 fl oz	$^1/_2$ cup
180 ml	6 fl oz	$^3/_4$ cup
250 ml	8 fl oz	1 cup
300 ml	10 fl oz ($^1/_2$ pint)	$1^1/_4$ cups
375 ml	12 fl oz	$1^1/_2$ cups
435 ml	14 fl oz	$1^3/_4$ cups
500 ml	16 fl oz	2 cups
625 ml	20 fl oz (1 pint)	$2^1/_2$ cups
750 ml	24 fl oz ($1^1/_5$ pints)	3 cups
1 litre	32 fl oz ($1^3/_5$ pints)	4 cups
1.25 litres	40 fl oz (2 pints)	5 cups
1.5 litres	48 fl oz ($2^2/_5$ pints)	6 cups
2.5 litres	80 fl oz (4 pints)	10 cups

DRY MEASURES

Metric	Imperial
30 grams	1 ounce
45 grams	$1^1/_2$ ounces
55 grams	2 ounces
70 grams	$2^1/_2$ ounces
85 grams	3 ounces
100 grams	$3^1/_2$ ounces
110 grams	4 ounces
125 grams	$4^1/_2$ ounces
140 grams	5 ounces
280 grams	10 ounces
450 grams	16 ounces (1 pound)
500 grams	1 pound, $1^1/_2$ ounces
700 grams	$1^1/_2$ pounds
800 grams	$1^3/_4$ pounds
1 kilogram	2 pounds, 3 ounces
1.5 kilograms	3 pounds, $4^1/_2$ ounces
2 kilograms	4 pounds, 6 ounces

LENGTH

Metric	Imperial
0.5 cm	$^1/_4$ inch
1 cm	$^1/_2$ inch
1.5 cm	$^3/_4$ inch
2.5 cm	1 inch

OVEN TEMPERATURE

	°C	°F	Gas Regulo
Very slow	120	250	1
Slow	150	300	2
Moderately slow	160	325	3
Moderate	180	350	4
Moderately hot	190/200	370/400	5/6
Hot	210/220	410/440	6/7
Very hot	230	450	8
Super hot	250/290	475/550	9/10

ABBREVIATION

tsp	teaspoon
Tbsp	tablespoon
g	gram
kg	kilogram
ml	millilitre